The Unstoppable Woman's Guide to Emotional Well-Being

A book for women written by unstoppable female authors, coaches, and professionals to help you establish and maintain emotional wellness.

Published By:
Unstoppable Publishing
13553 South Cicero Ave #176
Crestwood, IL. 60445
866-443-6769

Cover Design:
LaChapelle Design Works
Lachapelledesign.com

Interior Editing Also By:
Tina A. Swain, Lead Editor of Imani Publishing
Imani Publishing
www.imanipublishing.net

ISBN: 978-0-9838223-1-8

Other books available for purchase in the
Unstoppable Woman's Library:

10 Ways to Prevent Failure (Audio Book)
*A straight-forward guide to help you stay focused
on attaining your goals.*

Starting Today
*365 quotations to stimulate, inspire, and enhance
your personal growth.*

The Secrets to Being an Unstoppable Woman
*How to roll up your sleeves, make no excuses,
and get what you want!*

How to Write & Publish Your Book Now!!

www.ErikaGilchrist.com
866-443-6769
info@erikagilchrist.com

FOREWORD

Have you ever been around a group of really powerful women? And I'm not just talking about women who have long titles in front or behind their names. I'm talking about the energy you feel when you're surrounded by women who are so sure of themselves – so sure about who they are and who they are meant to be. It's stunning, isn't it? And somehow just by being in their presence you feel more empowered, inspired, and determined to take charge of your life.

If you haven't had the chance to experience that before…get ready. It's what this book is all about. Erika Gilchrist has done a fabulous job of getting these dynamic women to share their words of wisdom on how YOU can become an emotionally sound unstoppable woman.

Most women are already great human beings. We're innately wonderful. We're the matriarchs of our families, communities and of our own lives. But, what's an *Unstoppable* woman? I'm glad you asked. It's the difference between being ordinary and being *extraordinary*. It's the difference between moving through life and really *living it*. It's the difference between making a difference and being *legendary*.

As you read these pages, let yourself feel the energy and vigor resonating from each woman, each story, and each lesson. And prepare to become…*an Unstoppable Woman!*

Maya Watson
Marketing Manager, Harpo Studios

The Editor

Erika Gilchrist, *"The Unstoppable Woman,"* is regarded as one of the most energizing, engaging, and captivating speakers in the industry. Her seminars, trainings, and keynotes have empowered thousands of people. A partial list of corporations, associations, and universities that have attended Erika's speaking engagements include: Monster (.com), Target, Enterprise Rent ⟨ Car, and Mississippi Valley State University. Growing up ᴠ ʰh traumatic beginnings has not only taught her how to adapt ᵗᵒ change, but also how to overcome adversity. Erika is a Chicago native and during her youth, she has witnessed firsthand the effects that gang violence, drug abuse, and poverty has had on her community. As a result, she developed a strong passion for empowering women to overcome barriers to make them unstoppable in their own lives. Despite challenging surroundings during her formative years, Erika has achieved great success. Some of her accomplishments include:

- 2007 Highest Trainer Rating of the Year on 'Conflict Management Skills for Women' by SkillPath Seminars
- Published author of three books: Starting Today, 10 Ways to Prevent Failure, & The Secrets to Being an Unstoppable Woman
- Former on-air radio personality on WKKC 89.3 FM Chicago
- Owner of Unstoppable Publishing Company

Erika travels across the globe giving keynote speeches that inspire her audiences to move into action. "It's important to me to provide people with tangible and practical techniques that they can implement right away; not in six months, or a year from now, but things that can be done *right now* to begin that process."

www.ErikaGilchrist.com - info@erikagilchrist.com - 866-443-6769

Table of Contents

 Susan Tolles is the founder and creator of Flourish Over 50® and Powerful Me™, inspiring and equipping women around the world to live healthy, balanced lives as they discover that "life doesn't end after 50." After devoting her own life to family and community service, Susan reached a crossroads and found herself wondering, "Now what?" She wanted to be productive while doing something she truly enjoyed, so she began a period of exploration and renewal. Soon, she was energized by the countless women she encountered and their stories of reinvention and success. This, in turn, inspired her to create a place and program empowering women to create their own dream-come-true lives.

As a Certified Dream Coach®, website creator and writer, Susan Tolles is passionately living out her Life Purpose Statement: *To lead women to embrace their passion, purpose and power for extraordinary lives.* Her website FlourishOver50.com, viewed by thousands of women in 92 countries, gives them the resources and tools to live life to the fullest, including articles on style, health & fitness, life balance and transitions. As a Certified Dream Coach®, Susan leads women through her Powerful Me™ Program which she created to help them design a road map for their own extraordinary future. Susan lives in Austin, Texas with her husband of 32 years, Jim. They have three exceptional adult children and two Malti-poos.

Contact information:
13505 Byrd's Nest Drive
Austin, Texas 78738
512-797-2438
susan@flourishover50.com
http://flourishover50.com
http://mypowerfulme.com

Chapter 1

Work & Home: Striking the Right Balance
by: Susan Tolles

Do you live your life in overdrive, striving for perfection in everything you do? Is your life defined by what you have accomplished in your career? Does your work consume your days, leaving you little time to do the things you love?

If you are like most women, you are trying to be "superwoman," juggling work, home and family, while trying to manage the universe. Instead of living in alignment with what brings *you* joy and self-fulfillment, you may be living to serve everyone else, sacrificing your own happiness along the way. You may be so driven in your mission that you have lost sight of what the true goal is – to live fully every day, with a life that is vibrant, balanced and meaningful. Your identity may be wrapped up in your "doing" instead of your "being." You simply have lost focus.

I speak with authority on this subject, because I've "been there, done that," more than once. Not long ago, I reached a major crossroads in my life as an "Empty Nester" who had poured my mind, body and soul into raising my three children for 25 years. I had been a "supermom," volunteering in our schools, acting as room mother to the school board president, all the time taking pride in knowing that my role as "mom" was my identity. But, when my children were grown and left home, reality hit – who was I? I began my search for something new to do, something that would fill my need to be productive, while still fun and rewarding. That's when I stepped out of my comfort zone and, instead of going to work for someone, I created my own new career. In February of 2010, I launched a website for women over 50, responding to my own need to find great resources to live abundantly as I "aged," not accepting the myth that being over 50 meant that life was really over. FlourishOver50.com soon became my identity, and I worked night and day to make it successful. I was fueled by the response I received from women around the world. I was on a path to a career as the "Founder of Flourish Over 50" and that would be my identity when I was 80 years old, or so I thought.

At the end of the first year, I was exhausted. I had been so driven to develop and nurture the website, that I was overworked, overstressed and totally out of balance. Instead of spending evenings with my husband enjoying our newfound free time, I would sit with the computer in my lap as we watched TV or as he read. I suddenly realized that I didn't have a clear plan for the future, and began to question if I was even *on* the right path. I needed to focus on where I was *supposed* to go, not where I *assumed* my career would take me. It was time for me to stop, seek wisdom through prayer, find guidance from those who had gone before me, and get my own life in balance.

After spending some time studying the principles of success from experts Steven Covey, Jack Canfield, Brian Tracy and others, I understood what living fully really meant, and what it would take to get me there. My life was re-energized, and I began living with a renewed passion and a grander vision than I ever would have imagined, even a year ago. Inspired by my own self-guided transformation, I created a program called *Powerful Me*™ that helps women create a roadmap for a life filled with purpose and clarity. Through this program, combined with the Flourish Over 50® website, I equip women to live healthy, balanced lives in midlife and beyond, to dream big and step out on faith as they create an extraordinary future. I can't say today that I have conquered the challenge of keeping my work and home lives perfectly balanced, but I am getting closer all the time, and I have learned that keeping on track depends largely on one primary thing: **FOCUS**.

- **<u>Fill your own cup first, and then give away what flows over to the saucer.</u>** This is very likely the hardest thing for women to do, because we are natural givers and want to ensure everyone else is happy and well cared for. We become physically, emotionally and spiritually depleted as we live in service to others. Eventually we collapse, drained and depressed. You **must** learn to look out for **you** first by engaging in self-care daily. A healthy body will give you the energy you need to accomplish your goals, a healthy mind will keep you sharp and focused, and a healthy spiritual life will provide wisdom and direction. Proper nourishment in each of these areas will provide abundant energy to share in your personal and professional life. You cannot give away what you don't have, so make sure you are filled to overflowing. Here are some handy tips:

    o   Start your morning focused on what you need to feel happy and fulfilled. Pray, meditate and ask for guidance in planning your day. Get some exercise and eat a healthy breakfast to energize your body and fuel your brain.

    o Allow yourself some "me time" on a regular basis. Unplug, get away for some peace and quiet, and relax. Step away and do the things you enjoy, because the more relaxed and refreshed you are, the more productive and content you will be.

o   Don't deprive yourself of sleep. Even one or two extra hours of sleep every night will make a huge difference in your days. Make a commitment to go to bed earlier and see how much better you feel every morning, awaking rested instead of tired.

o   Remember to *breathe* along the way. There really is a science behind breathing deeply to give you energy and clarity. If you are like most people, you breathe shallowly and irregularly, using only 20% of your lung capacity. But breathing in deeply through your nose, holding it for seven seconds, then exhaling through your mouth actually increases oxygen saturation, clearing the mind, purifying the blood, providing more energy and calming the body. On the other hand, lack of oxygen will lead to mental sluggishness, lack of focus, depression and anxiety. Practice this breathing exercise several times a day, inhaling and exhaling three times slowly, concentrating on taking in energy-giving oxygen while exhaling your stress.

- **Organize your life around what brings you joy and satisfaction.** What are you doing that you love to do? What are you doing that, if given the chance; you wouldn't even begin in the first place? Take a hard look at the things that are really important to you and make those your priorities. *Stop* doing the things that bring you down. If you design a life based on your core passions, values and desires, you will live with meaning and happiness. If your life is based on what others want for you, your life will be filled with stress and dissatisfaction. Embrace your life purpose and stand in the power of who you are now, and who you will become as you design your own future.

o   Define your Life Purpose Statement, your own personal mission statement for your future. According to Stephen Covey, author of *The Seven Habits of Highly Effective People*, "Creating a Personal Mission Statement will be, without question, one of the most powerful and significant things you will ever do to take leadership of your life … all the goals and decisions you will make in the future will be based upon it."

o   Set some top priorities for yourself, the things that are non-negotiable in your life, things that ultimately will make you a better person. Of course, "self care" should be high on the list! These are the areas of your life that you *want* to spend 80% of your time on as you live your abundant future, in alignment with your core values and desires.

o   Establish clear goals that support your life purpose and priorities. Make them high enough to push you past your "comfort zone," but not so high that you will fail, no matter how hard you try. Know that accomplishing your goals will propel you toward a more fulfilled joyful life.

- **Control your calendar and your inbox.** If you remain focused on your Life Purpose, priorities and goals as you set your schedule, your days will be more productive and satisfying. If you get off-track and let others distract you, you will reach the end of each day frustrated and unproductive. Internationally respected leadership authority Dr. Steven Covey says, "The key is not to prioritize what's on your schedule, but to schedule your priorities." Manage your calendar, don't let it manage you.

14

o   See how much white space you can leave on your daily planner, not how much you can cover up.

o   Plan your meetings and luncheons on certain days, leaving one or two days a week free from outside responsibilities. These will be *your* days to focus on your own goals, and to get caught up on emails and phone calls.

o   Don't get bogged down with checking your email early in the day. Author and expert teacher Brendon Burchard says that your email is a convenient organizing tool for other people's agendas. A recent study found that the average American with a smart phone checks it 34 times every day. Just think of the time you are wasting by not being focused on *your own* agenda! If it is really urgent, you will get a phone call, not an email.

o   Schedule your daily to-do list according to urgency and importance. If too many things have a high priority, run through the list again and demote the less important ones. Once you have done this, rewrite the list in priority order.

You might put them in a grid like this:

	Urgent	Not Urgent
Important	**MANAGE: Critical to achieving goals** Time sensitive projects, reports Crisis situations Medical emergencies Last-minute preparations	**FOCUS: Important to achieving goals** Relationship-building Strategic planning Self-care Recreation/relaxation
Not Important	**USE CAUTION: Interruptions** Checking email constantly Some phone calls Other people's agendas, expectations "Administrivia"	**AVOID: Distractions** Social media, unless used in business development Some phone calls Surfing the internet Television

- **Understand that you have choices, not obligations.** There is great freedom in saying "no," so do it often! Choose the things that give you energy and support your goals. Focus on the things that are truly important, and don't feel guilty about being protective of your time. Remember, when you say "no" to one thing, your time will be freed up to say "yes" to something else.

  o Use your Life Purpose Statement, priorities and goals to evaluate every opportunity you are presented. If the task/job/event does not align with your core purpose, then gracefully say "no."

  o Realize that if you say "no," that allows someone else to say "yes," and that person may delight in the opportunity, not dread it.

o   Say to yourself, "If I do this, what will I not be doing? How will that affect my progress in accomplishing my to-do list?"

o   If it is not a clear "YES" then it is a "NO." If you don't feel a sense of certainty about making a commitment, then it is not right for you. Trust your intuition.

- **<u>Separate your work life and personal life with clear boundaries.</u>** Set a clear schedule for your day, work diligently, and then *quit* when the time is up. Few projects require you to spend your nights and weekends away from your personal life. If you have a job that takes up most of your time, then consider a change. Answer this question: If you knew you only had six months to live, what would you do more of? Chances are you didn't say "work!" Spend more time doing the things you love, and know that your work is a means to achieving a great life, not the other way around.

    o   If your career takes you to an office, then breathe deeply when you arrive home and be "present" with everyone who is there. Unwind and enjoy visiting about your day instead of continuing it in your study or at the kitchen table.

    o   If you work at home, turn off the computer, shut the door, and pretend that you have driven 10 miles. Step outside for your "commute time" and get some fresh air as you end your workday.

    o   Focus on your relationships, enjoy the things that

17

enrich your life, and know that the tasks that didn't get accomplished one day will be there the next. No one will care that you waited a few hours to get them done.

o   Try keeping a journal for two weeks, writing down the time you spend every day in work, free time, sleep, eating and chores, and "miscellaneous" time that includes checking phone and email messages, Facebook and watching TV. Everyone has the same 24 hours in each day. How are you spending yours? Where are you wasting time? What needs to be rebalanced for a more fulfilled life?

We have all been trained that to be effective we must be ultra-productive and work long hours. In reality, working long hours drains precious energy and joy from our lives and ultimately keeps us from experiencing true happiness. It doesn't come easily or quickly but with practice, living a balanced life will become the norm and you will experience life with more contentment and energy than ever before. Start now getting more FOCUS and you, too, will find greater success in your work life, and more time to do the things that are really important to you. You will be unstoppable!

Luz is an accomplished Nurse Clinical Educator, Master Coach, Motivational Speaker, Instructor and Counselor, Health Advocate, Consultant and Registered Nurse. She has 30 years success as a "driving force' in healthcare and health education, meeting challenges, setting standards and generating improvements through system changes and training.

Luz is also a Reiki Master, a Clinical Hypnotherapist, a Past Life Regression Therapist, and a Spiritual Instructor (Free Soul Organization). She holds certifications as a Health and Wellness Coach, Spiritual Coach, NLP Coach, Group Coach, Life Coach and Master Coach. She has created workshops, classes, and retreats for health care providers and the general public.

Luz is the president and owner of Integrated Holistic Concepts. She is dedicated to helping people achieve their goals and dreams emotionally, physically, and spiritually through Coaching, EFT, Reiki, Integrative Health Modalities, Travel, and Business.

Luz's success is built on the ability to inspire teamwork and tap into the unique expertise of others. She is a strong believer in lifelong learning. She is uniquely qualified to present a continuum of information from traditional medicine to holistic healing that provides people the choices to include more self-care and wellness in their lives. As her life experiences sit at the crossroads of traditional medicine and holistic wellness with 30 years of experience as a highly credentialed nurse, and over 25 years of spirituality experience and teaching, she can see both sides: the worldly and the spiritual.

Contact information:
Luz@IntegratedHolisticConcepts.com
www.IntegratedHolisticConcepts.com
www.MySparePaycheck.com

Chapter 2

7 Stress Solutions for Women
by: Luz N. Adams

You know the negative effects of stress on your body and in your life. But what is important to manage stress is to take control: to take charge of your emotions, your thoughts, your problems, and yourself. While there are many ways to take charge of your life and to create solutions to deter stress, we will focus on seven solutions and tools to reduce stress and foster wellness. Most of the suggestions are fun, simple, and easy to do.

Why seven? Ponder this…

➢ There are 7 days in a week: Monday, Tuesday, Wednesday, Thursday, Friday, Saturday, and Sunday

➢ There are 7 directions: Right, Left, Up, Down, Forward, Backward, and Center

➢ There are 7 musical notes: Do, Re, Mi, Fa, So, La, Ti

➢ There are 7 colors in the rainbow: Red, Orange, Yellow, Green, Blue, Indigo, and Purple

➢ There are 7 senses: Vision, Hearing, Touch, Taste, Smell, Emotional, and Spiritual

➢ There are 7 chakras: Root, Sacral, Solar Plexus, Heart, Throat, Third Eye, and Crown

➢ There are 7 major Archangels: Ariel, Gabriel, Jophiel, Michael, Raphael, Uriel, and Zadkiel

➢ There are 7 wonders of the Ancient World, and 7 wonders of the Modern World.

And there are many Power Words with 7 letters: Rainbow, Harmony, Thought, Breathe, Sunning, Synergy, Stretch, Writing, Dessert, Purpose, Realize, Achieve, Imagine, Winners, Natural,

Believe, Inspire, Therapy, Healthy, Perfect, Finance, Destiny, Success, and Seventh. You can probably think of many more. Which ones speak to you?

Seven is considered a sacred or mystic number. In numerology, seven is focused on "thought" and it is considered the most spiritual of all numbers representing spiritual perfection and completeness. The Bible teaches that God completed his work and on the 7th day He rested. It is said that the seventh day or Sabbath is the day that represents rest. Therefore, we will use 7 areas with solutions or tools to allow our mind, body, and soul to de-stress so you can rest and rejuvenate.

In your conscious effort to take charge of your emotions, your thoughts, your problems, and yourself, these solutions/tools serve as a beautiful personal rainbow. As you look at your personal rainbow, notice that each area, solution, or color is separate. Together, all the colors and areas create a perfect work of art. <u>YOU</u>.

Let's look at these areas for you to take charge of your life. See where they can work individually or separately and notice that when they are working together how they create your masterpiece:

1. Breathing and Light
2. Touch
3. Visualization
4. Music and Rhythm
5. Movement
6. Ritual
7. Inspiration

1. Breathing and Light

The most important and easiest way to de-stress is by breathing. While we normally do not consciously think about breathing, most of us do not breathe well or deep enough. It is time to consciously think about your breathing, especially if you are feeling stressed. When was the last time you took a really, really, deep breath? It is easy, it can be done anywhere, and nobody needs to know. Just now as you are reading, take a deep breath... and let it out, again, take another deep breath, and another one. Try taking a deep breath slowly in through your nose. Pull that breath deep down in your belly, past your belly-button. Then slowly, exhale completely through your mouth. Do this three times. Notice how you feel calmer. Great, that's a start. Wasn't that really easy? The results are wondrous; your body fills with oxygen. Oxygen "is your life force" and we need to continuously and consciously take deeper breaths. Slower and deeper, these great deep breaths calm down the nervous system that is firing up your cells, your thoughts, and your emotions. You can also consciously use your deep breaths when you meditate, to lower your blood pressure and heart rate to calm yourself down. You can take just a minute to de-stress with breathing. You can do it while you are in line at a busy supermarket or the bank, in a board room, in the bathroom, or while cooking or exercising. It is available to you on command. So why don't you take some more deep breathes right now? Consider taking a daily deep breath bath, or several breathing baths, throughout the day.

Here are a few fun exercises you can try.

Exercise 1

Breathe in, close your eyes, and imagine a large amount of oxygen molecules traveling everywhere in your body and filling every area and space in your body, starting with your head and your brain... oxygen bubbles filling all your

senses... filling your eyes, ears, nose, mouth. These armies of oxygen molecules are filled with love, light, and life force in the form of oxygen, and the more oxygen they release the more they produce. The more you breathe in deeply, the more molecules enter your body. Be aware of these oxygen bubbles as they move down to your throat, lungs, and heart, filling these areas with love, oxygen, and life. Feel your lungs expand, and feel your heart beat as these happy bubbles move down to your stomach, internal organs, liver, pancreas, spleen, kidneys, intestines, and continue down your legs to your ankles, and your feet. In your mind's eye, look back at yourself and your body's reflection. What do you see? The beautiful being that you are is filled with oxygen, life, light, and love; shining brightly, a being of light and fluid oxygen that is healthy, whole, complete and relaxed. Smile. Give thanks.

Exercise 2

Your daily oxygen bath:
As you take your daily shower, brush your teeth, or wash your hands, sense the water flowing over your body with those friendly oxygen molecules of love, light, peace, and relaxation. As you know, water is H_2O, two hydrogen molecules helping oxygen move about. Anything that is negative or stressful in your

body or your life, feel it being washed away from you. As it goes down the drain it turns into positive energy for the world and a lightness, healing and relaxation flows over you.

One more thought on water, we have all been told to drink plenty. Our bodies are made up mostly of water. Our thoughts are energy and we drink fluid oxygen in the form of water to cleanse the energy, to reenergize our being, and to be healthy. So how does water reduce stress? It is very simple; imagine your body is a fish tank. You must change the water frequently and place a filter with oxygen bubbles for the fish tank to be pristine and sparkle, right? Well, the same goes for your body and your soul. Water is a solution. Filtered water is even better!

Other Tools

Light therapy, along with breathing, is an easy tool to use to de-stress. You can also use aromatherapy in combination with your breathing. Now you can easily combine the two with a few colorful and aromatic candles. Lavender is a very calming and soothing aroma and color. You can use the power of color to adjust your mood, calm down, and de-stress. It is as simple as the color of the clothing you choose each day. Shades of blue are calming. Green is a healing color. Pink is the color of love. Red is the color of energy. Yellow is the color of happiness. White is the color of light. Purple is the color of spirituality. Brown and black are the colors of grounding.

Gold and Silver are colors of purpose. Notice the colors around you and the message they are sending you.

You can use light therapy to meditate, to de-stress, for healing, and for manifesting things in your life. It is as simple as having the picture of a rainbow in your cubicle at work, or in your bedroom or bath and concentrate on the color you need for a few minutes. You can do the same with colored candles. To emanate the energy you desire, use the color coding in the previous paragraph. I particularly do not like to use any Brown or Black candles, as I do not like the energy they emanate. A better solution for grounding is to garden or go into nature and work with the natural greens and browns in the plants and soil.

2. The Power of Touch

A caress, an embrace, a kiss, a smile, a hug, a walk in nature, a massage, and stopping to smell the flowers, all are tools that use the power of touch. How can you touch someone and how can they touch you? It can be as simple as a smile. Try this... smile at a stranger when they least expect it and notice their reaction. Now, notice your body's reaction. Smile at a child and notice how you feel when they smile back. Usually it's at this point when you realize that you have been touched. Notice how you soften and open. There are many tools that can be used to de-stress using the power of touch. Start by looking in the mirror and smiling at you. In fact, do this every day.

A very easy tool is the power of massage. You can do it daily or many times a day. The touching tools to use are your hands and your feet. While it is a wonderful feeling to get a body massage and to spend a day at the spa, time and money often limit such pleasures. But did you know that your hands and feet are filled with the end points of what are called meridians? A meridian is an energy pathway in your body that carries vital life force throughout your body and your internal organs. We are used to applying lotion to our hands and feet, after a bath, and throughout the day. This is your perfect opportunity to give yourself a fast, inexpensive, relaxing and revitalizing massage using your hands.

The official terminology for this type of massage is reflexology. As you apply your lotion you can apply pressure to your fingertips to reduce sinus pressure, apply pressure or massage to the fleshy part between your index and middle finger to relieve head pressure and tension, or to the side of the hands to relieve tension in your back. My suggestion is to get a very inexpensive reflexology pocket card. They can be purchased at whole food stores or alternative therapy stores. Learn the areas in your hands and feet that correlate to the parts of your body experiencing stress. You can also look on-line for hand and feet reflexology maps. Every time you apply lotion to your hands or feet give yourself a free and beneficial massage. Better yet, get a group of friends and have a hand massage party, where everyone gives and gets a hand massage. Always do both hands for balancing the left and right sides of the body.

1. **Sinuses**
2. **Eyes**
3. **Ears**
4. **Shoulder**
5. **Liver**
6. **Gall Bladder**
7. **Throat**
8. **Colon**
9. **Bladder**
10 . **Lower Lumbar**

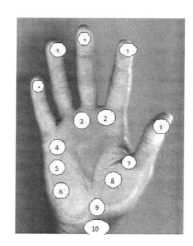

If you are interested in the power of touch, you can learn about reflexology, massage and Reiki on the Worldwide Web. There is a lot of information about these topics on the internet.

3. Visualization/Meditation

Visualization and Meditation does not always come easy for everyone. Most people think that you need to stop what you are doing for one hour or so to enjoy a good meditation. Another misconception is that you need to sit cross-legged and chant as if you were in a temple to meditate. Broaden your understanding to observe that meditation occurs whenever you are quiet and calm. People meditate when they walk, sew, pray, read, exercise, and do many other tasks. This is also a simple and easy tool to add to your life. There are many ways to meditate and visualize.

The best word to describe visualization is imagination. Most of us have lost our ability to imagine, dream, make believe, or create new realities in our lives. You are the master of your destiny whether you believe it or not. Henry Ford said, "If you believe you can't or if you believe you can, you are right." So choose to believe you can. Some people have a hard time visualizing because they cannot see very well with their mind's eye, and that is OK. It is a skill you can develop, but for now, just try to sense and believe.

Here's an exercise that I call my walking meditation. Take five minutes out of your busy day, whether from work, your household chores, or a stressful day. Preferably walk on green grass, or at a park, but anyplace will do. Consciously, go for a walk with yourself. Take some deep breaths and imagine your best friend walking with you, that friend is an identical clone of yourself. Engage in a friendly and loving conversation. Tell your best friend (self) what is on your mind, stressing you out. Take about a minute or two as you continue to walk and do not stop walking, even if it is baby steps. Just listen to your friend give you answers and advice, without interrupting your friend. Breathe deeply as you listen to yourself give answers to you. If you prefer, you can use your Angels, Guides, or God. You can visualize this as you walk,  or just sense that wise part of yourself that has the answers and is able to give you advice. You can do this technique as often as you want; if you have more than five minutes, then do it for ten or twenty. At the beginning, it might feel silly listening to yourself, but as you get more used to your inner wisdom talking to you, you will start trusting the answers and advice.

Another visualization tool is called the "Life Movie." This tool might take a little longer but you can do it over and over. Change it as often as you want. It's your life. You are the director of this movie so you can edit, add, create, and imagine anything you want. It is YOUR movie. Close your eyes, and see a movie in your mind of your life or your actual situation. Imagine yourself in the director's chair and the editing room. Now change the scene to what you want your life or situation to be. Take a deep breath; say, "Cut...that's a wrap!" Start watching a whole new movie that you have created. If you change your mind about your movie and want a different ending, no problem. Do it again or as many times as you want. Once you are happy with the ending, start believing and know that you are the master of your destiny. We all create our lives every day. Create the life you'd love to live.

4. Music/Rhythm

This is a very easy tool to use. It does not matter what type of music you like, when you start feeling stressed, just listen to music. Music has the power to calm the spirit, to resonate in our bodies, and to make us feel lighter and happier. Notice the types of music you have available and choose music to create the effect you desire, whether calming or inspirational. Be aware that there is a category of music that is "engineered" to create calming and healing effects. Hemi-Sync is the producer of this music and can be found online. If you do not have music available to you, then sing, or hum your favorite tune. Humming is of great benefit, as it calms the mind, reduces stress, and calms the entire nervous system. It is also beneficial to your body and creates vibrations in your body that help you relax. You can easily hum a song, preferably a happy song, or the word OM or AUM. The sound of Om is also called Pranava, meaning that it sustains life and runs through prana or breath. Humming the word OM fills your body with energy, power and strength; you can also use this technique with your walking meditation.

Another very popular form of relaxation that is gaining popularity is drumming in the form of drumming circles. Whether you learn how to drum, or just use your hands as the instrument and concentrate on the vibrations of drumming, the studies are showing great results in decreasing the stress in your mind and body, and increasing physical and mental health benefits. Of course, indigenous cultures have known this since the dawn of time. A very soothing and easy exercise you can do is to find a quite place, take a deep breath, and listen to the rhythm of your heart beat, then with your hand on a table or a drum place that beat on that object. Concentrate on the speed and vibrations of your heart beat, continuing to breathe deeply and do it for as long as it takes to feel more relaxed.

5. Movement

 You have heard that exercise is a great way to de-stress, and there are many things you can do with this modality. You can run, swim, do yoga, tai-chi, qui-gong, or dancing. What is important is the fact that you give your body movement. Have you seen children listening to music start dancing? They just move their bodies any way they feel is right. We have a lot to learn from children. Along with the music tool, move or dance anyway that makes you feel good, anyway your body tells you to. Do not worry if it is right or not, just go with the flow. Relax and move, let yourself play as if you were a child again. Play is one of the most powerful de-stressing tools you have available.

Look for books, instructional videos or classes on yoga, tai-chi, or qui-gong and try one. Many of these can be found online for free. You might just find that it is exactly what you have been looking for.

6. Ritual and Prayer

It is amazing what power prayer has in our lives, our bodies, and our attitudes. There is no right or wrong way to pray. Just ask from your heart because God hears all prayers. Prayer can be your inner conversation with God. Pray, ask, be joyful. Always, always, give thanks for all your blessings. It has been said, "seven days without prayer, makes one weak." Prayer is talking and listening to God from your heart. Use some of the techniques we have discussed so far and add a few prayers. You'll be glad you did.

As far as ritual, have you ever wondered: why the British have tea and crumpets at 4 PM every day, why in Spain and some Latin American countries they take a "siesta" (nap) after lunch, and why the Native American people do Pow-Wows and pray around the medicine wheel and sweat lodge? It is all about ritual. Ritual helps you focus your mind, center your being, and heal. Ritual is focusing the intention of your thoughts around an action.

One suggestion is that you create your own ritual, which helps you relax. It could be that break for a cup of coffee or tea every day, it could be a relaxing bath after work or before you go to bed, it could be reading a book after the children are in bed, or bird watching every weekend. Take some time out for you.

7. Inspiration

Inspiration includes things such as writing, journaling, painting, laughing, and inspiring others. There is such a feeling of peace and accomplishment when you are of service to others in need. Feelings of strength and power arise when you create things whether you chose to share them with others or not.

As you recall, at the beginning of this chapter, I mentioned some 7-letter power words. A great exercise is for you to write a letter to yourself, from your inner being congratulating you on your dreams, goals, and successes but only using positive power words.

How many of those can you use? What is it that you have always wanted to acknowledge to yourself?

Let me help you start the letter dedicated to you. It may sound like this: Dear Child of God, today is a wonderful day. After the rain last night this morning you look like a **rainbow** of beauty. **Breathe** deeply, **imagine** and **realize** that you are **perfect,** and **healthy.**

31

You have **purpose** and **achieve** and **deserve success.** Try painting, drawing, or doodling, even if you think you can't, this is just for you. Can you use some of those seven letter words and express them in pictures or symbols? Does this come naturally to you?

We have covered seven areas to help you de-stress; you can use one or all of them. Some will appeal to you, and some will not. Once you start to apply these tools, others will present themselves for your consideration. The idea is that you use techniques that will help you take control of your life and become that unstoppable woman! Good luck!

 Jennifer "Jenny" Engle, an award winning marketing and communications professional and entrepreneur, is a popular speaker, trainer, and writer. As the owner and principal of jke marketing & communications, she is active in the for-profit and not-for-profit sectors. Her business, which is Green Plus Certified, focuses on sustainable practices involving people, planet, and performance.

Jenny is the author of numerous magazine and newspaper features. The Pennsylvania native enjoys social media and regularly blogs and writes on communicating professionally, perfecting your writing skills, building positive professional relationships, and strategic planning and positioning. She also is a judge for various international communications competitions and reviews and evaluates professional work portfolios for communications certification.

One of Pennsylvania's top 50 Women in Business and Central PA's 25 Women of Influence, Jenny is a platinum level member of WomenCentric Speakers Bureau, a trainer with MVP Seminars, an expert with Problem Solved Daily, and the past national president of the Association for Women in Communications. A former wine association executive, she also likes to de-snob the mysteries of the grape and introduce the joys of wine into colleagues' personal and professional lives.

A strong believer in lifelong learning, Jenny earned an MPA from Penn State University and a BS from Millersville University. She also is a Certified Communications Professional and speaks French and Spanish with a smattering of Mandarin Chinese.

Contact information:
www.jkecommunications.com
jenny@jkecommunications.com

Chapter 3

Be Your Own Cheerleader! (Self Motivation)
by: Jennifer K. Engle

After reading the title of this chapter, I bet you might be trying to visualize yourself as a cheerleader, right? Maybe some of you even were perky pompom pretties in your former life. For most of us, however, imagining ourselves bouncing around in short skirts and cheering on our favorite teams or sports stars is a real stretch. I know it is for me.

What I can visualize, and smile about, are the many different times I've enthusiastically cheered on my kids, my co-workers, friends, and family. I'm sure you've done this as well. Remember how you told them how wonderful, talented, creative, hardworking, caring, and generous they are? You encouraged them to learn from their failures and heartaches and not to listen to hurtful remarks from people who are so insecure, that they have to bring others down to make themselves feel good.

Whether you realized it or not, you've been their cheerleader. I bet, for the people you really care for, you'd gladly be a cheerleader everyday!

So, as an Unstoppable Woman, you are more than capable of recognizing and owning your self-worth. Remember that you deserve everything your heart desires if you are willing to work for it. Be your own advocate, and don't be afraid to visualize yourself wearing whatever outfits you choose to be the best cheerleader you can be. Remember, if you don't speak up for yourself, no one else will!

Bragging the Right Way

That said, there are definitely right and wrong ways to toot your own horn. You've heard those folks who feel they could extol their virtues forever. You remember them . . . but for all the wrong reasons.

I usually am rolling my eyes and looking for a way to escape when I hear speeches like this one:

> *"Jenny, I am number one in my field and I've won so many awards I've lost count. People are flocking to my door, and I can't keep up with the emails and calls. I've had to stop going to networking meetings because people overwhelm me with questions about my success. I don't have time to waste with most of these hangers on. I just keep moving forward looking for the diamond contacts that can help me get ahead."*

On the other hand, there is the person who puts a smile on your face because she is so passionate about what she does. This is an individual you would recommend or hire. Her speech might sound like this:

> *"Jenny, you know it's amazing how fortunate I've been in my career. I love what I do, and I get so excited about the prospect of helping someone grow their business. Usually, after carefully listening to a potential client, my juices get flowing and the creativity kicks in. I never know who or what might give me a good idea, so I enjoy connecting with many individuals. I love to*

go to meetings and network. I also enjoy sharing tips with people I meet. Giving back is just as rewarding as moving forward."

So, to which "Honker" would you prefer listening? Obviously, the first person would most likely make your eyes glaze over very quickly. Plus, I've generally found that someone who feels the need to brag about herself all the time is the one who is most insecure about her talents. She tends to berate others to make herself feel more important. Why is it we can recognize individuals like her in a heartbeat when she brings down others we care about, but we often have difficulty recognizing her shortcomings when she tries to work her mojo on us?

The second woman, however, makes her point in a pleasant and enthusiastic way that emphasizes her talents and strengths. You get a pretty good idea that this person has your interests at heart, and you're impressed.

Underdog to the Rescue
Another positive way to be your own cheerleader involves telling personal stories. Most of us have a soft spot for underdogs. Think about it. Who do you root for at various sports events and in the movies? Usually, it's the 97 pound weakling who's trying really hard, the horse that's had poor starts, the shy girl who isn't overtly pretty or outgoing, or the good guys who are outrageously outnumbered.

Like me, you've probably had some of those underdog moments – times when you've been overwhelmed with negative feelings or circumstances, times when you felt you couldn't compete, or times when you royally screwed up. Maybe you feel like an underdog right now.

Whatever your experiences as an underdog, use them to build relationships and let people know you're a problem solver! You didn't wallow in self pity. You picked yourself up, crawled out of that hole and learned from your mistakes. You've always tried to keep moving forward. Being an Unstoppable Woman is about making connections. So, share your stories and allow people to connect with you. We love to root for the underdog, and everyone loves a good story.

Show Them Your Smarts
In the second conversation example earlier in this chapter, my friend said that giving back is just as rewarding as moving forward. It may be even more so. You possess lots of knowledge. Really, you do. Whether you want to be a successful business woman, a top chef, a sought after hair stylist, or a wonderful homemaker, you can brag about all the knowledge and experience you have via social media. Best of all, you can do it without looking like you're bragging (like the woman in the first example).

You can share clever tips you've learned on Facebook. Better yet, create your own blog and share your viewpoints and advice as well as those pithy pointers. Offer thoughtful and/or helpful comments on other blogs too. They may ask you to write a guest blog as a bonus. Also try Tweeting about articles or books that have inspired you. Join LinkedIn groups that interest you and share comments or help someone else with their problems. Design your own page on Google + (FYI, it's now open to everyone), and begin forming your own circles of influence!

Social media is a great way to be your own cheerleader without outwardly saying you're incredibly talented. People will be impressed by your knowledge and know how, you smarty pants, you!

Getting On the Motivation Track

Now that you're feeling more comfortable with being your own cheerleader, it's time to get motivated to reach your goals. There's no one who can do a better job at motivating you than YOU! You'll feel the weight getting lighter on your shoulders as you work your way through the small stuff and make steady progress on the bigger projects.

We all have times when we feel lazy and unmotivated. Whatever the reason – work is boring, there's a project we don't want to complete, the weather's dreary, we can't face another uncomfortable meeting with family or friends, or we're just plain afraid to do something – staying in bed or kicking back and vegging out in our pjs seems like the best way to hide from the world. Maybe we'll watch movies or catch up on our favorite TV shows or read a book. My daughter calls these breaks her very necessary mental health days. They are perfectly normal, and all of us deserve a few of those breathers every now and then.

Problems develop when you allow insecurities, laziness and fear (**F**orget **E**verything **A**nd **R**un!) to keep you from getting things done and/or reaching your goals. You're probably thinking, "What goals?" But, in your heart of hearts, you know there are many goals you've consciously and subconsciously set for yourself. Maybe you've just called them hopes to make situations seem more acceptable if you don't reach them. But I'm telling you right now, you, as an Unstoppable Woman should set high goals for yourself – right from the start. (You deserve everything your heart desires – if you're willing to work for it.) Plus, you should tell people about your goals. Let those friends and colleagues in your Power Circle know too. The more people you tell (in a confident manner), the more difficult it will be for you **not** to try and succeed. Believe me, there will be days when you'll need all the positive encouragement you can get. There will also be times when you'll need the people you trust and respect to tell you to get your butt moving, stop making excuses or work harder.

Make Those Goals

Right now, take some time to think about three goals you really want to achieve in the next year. Think big and think positively. Write them down on the chart below. Don't worry about the phrasing, you can always make some changes later.

My goals

Are you starting to feel the excitement? Now that they are down on paper and in front of you, they are real. If you've been honest with yourself, you should be feeling the excitement building. Good things **are** possible.

Let's say your goals might be:

• Get promoted to Director of Marketing
• Lose 50 pounds
• Begin dating again.

Does each one of these goals take you outside your comfort zone? They probably should. Are they arranged in priority order? Can you work on them one at a time or would it be better to try to move forward with each simultaneously? Now, think again about why you wrote down your specific goals.

What motivates you to achieve them? Is it a need to demonstrate your love? Is it money, a desire to be healthy, the opportunity to share with others, the chance to build positive relationships, an aspiration to lead, the wish to further your education, or a yearning to find someone special? You may have multiple motivations for one or more of your goals, so write them beside each specific one. As an example, your sheet may look something like the following chart:

Goals	Motivation(s)
1. Lose 50 pounds	Be more healthy, look better
2. Begin dating again	Meet new people, have fun
3. Get promoted to Director of Marketing	I deserve it, lead others, share knowledge

On the surface, your goals may not seem to be related. But, look closer. Wouldn't each one help to build your confidence and self esteem? Won't that help to motivate you to keep moving forward?

You Can Do It

Now, visualize yourself achieving your goals --- 50 pounds thinner, dating again and working as Director of Marketing. To make this easier, you may want to cut or print out some pictures from magazines or the internet to help in that visualization process. Post them some place where you will see them often.

You may feel intimidated by your goals from time to time. Don't worry, that's natural. Breaking them down into bite sized pieces often makes them easier to handle. For instance, focus on losing five pounds or getting out once a month, or finishing one important project on time and under budget. Almost everything is more doable in small increments. Plus, those small victories are great motivators to keep you moving towards achieving your larger goals!

Make some time each day to positively focus on what you want to achieve that day. Don't be lazy or make excuses! You *can* find a few minutes. Perhaps the best time is when you're driving to work, sitting on a bus or metro, waiting in line for a cup of coffee, or even running the vacuum cleaner. I do some of my best visualizing on the treadmill or elliptical machine and in the shower. I also have many of the best cheerleader conversations with myself while driving. (I have Bluetooth in my car, so I figure people will just think I'm talking on the phone!) On rough days, there's nothing wrong with having several "chats with me" during the day – silently or aloud. Whatever works best for you and keeps you motivated. Make those few minutes count.

When I'm having a rough time finishing a project or I've had some tough feedback, I think of the book *The Help* by Kathryn Stockett. In it, the central character Aibileen tells the little girl whom she raises, "You is smart, you is beautiful and you is important." She tells her this over and over. When the little girl's mother constantly berates her for falling short of her expectations or doing something wrong, Aibileen hugs her and asks, "What do I tell you little girl?" Then, she repeats, "I am smart, I am beautiful, I am important." We never know for sure, but I think that girl must have repeated that phrase to herself many times over the years – and I bet it really motivated her to become successful. Each of us is smart, beautiful and important in our own special way, and we need to remember it.

Keep Your Eyes on the Prize

Don't forget to check in with your co-workers and your friends or family, with whomever you've shared your goals. Give them regular progress reports. (Think about this as if you were going to Weight Watchers or Jenny Craig and checking in with one of their consultants. It holds you accountable and makes it harder for you to come up short.) They can cheer you on and offer additional encouragement. They can also give you honest feedback if things aren't going as well as you hoped.

Goals	Motivations	Milestones/ Dates
1. Lose 50 pounds	Be more healthy, look better	Minus 5 lbs. 6/30
2. Begin dating again	Meet new people, have fun	First date 6/12
3. Get promoted to Director of Marketing	I deserve it, lead others, share knowledge	Good review 7/8

Enlarge your goal chart and include milestones and dates. Setbacks may happen, but don't let them hold you back. Stay focused. Unstoppable Women do not let obstacles keep them from moving ahead. They may need to make detours or take different paths to achieve their goals, but their motivation seldom lags. Remember, those small victories are still victories, and they add up to larger successes!

Knowing yourself, your strengths and weaknesses, as well as what motivates you, makes being your own cheerleader a snap. You go, girl!

Darlene Templeton is the CEO and founder of Templeton & Associates. She specializes in transformation and transition specifically for those who want to make a greater impact personally and professionally while rekindling their passion and drive for life. Darlene engages, inspires and empowers women who are overworked and overwhelmed, helping them to put more time back into their lives, so that can do the things that they truly love.

Darlene brings almost 36 years of extensive experience with one of the largest global corporation in the world. She is an executive coach, recognized leader and change agent who brings with her a wealth of experience, including 30 years of management, in the corporate world. She is an "out of the box" thinker and uses her skill to inspire business professionals toward extraordinary results. Fueled by her passion and enthusiasm, Darlene provides clients, teams and organizations alike, the tools for leadership, personal and professional excellence.

She has worked with many organizations and professionals to drive change through leadership and coaching. Darlene is a Certified Professional Co-active Coach (PCC) through The Coaches Training Institute, an Associate Certified Coaching and member of the International Coach Federation (ICF), and a Certified Dream Coach.

Darlene lives in Austin, Texas with her husband, John. She loves spending time with her family and her four grandchildren.

Contact information:
www.darlenetempleton.com
darlene@darlenetempleton.com

Chapter 4
Handling High Stakes Situations
by: Darlene Templeton

Have you ever felt like you are a player in the high stakes "World Championship Tournament of Poker" and that every hand is a "million dollar" hand? Did you feel that every decision you make could be life changing?

We all face huge challenges in our lives, whether it's a high level executive meeting in our business, the family drama that we face with aging or ill parents, or a child who is failing in school. We feel like the weight of the world is on our shoulders and that we must make the "right" decision, take the right action, or the consequences will be huge. I have felt that many times in my personal and professional life.

I completely understand, in fact I have even considered myself the "champion" of high stakes poker. When I look back over the years, I was in some type of "high stakes situation" professionally and personally my entire life. I just retired from one of the largest global corporations in the world, after an amazing and challenging career of almost 36 years. I climbed the ladder very quickly and was in management for 30 years of my career. The decisions that I made professionally affected so many people, and each one felt like a "million dollar" hand. I have fired people, told them they weren't performing, told them they will have to leave the company and have managed very difficult and extremely high-profile customer situations. In one situation, we were working with a customer who had a Department of Defense clearance, and I had to sign a contract on behalf of my company that said if we didn't deliver the equipment on time, I was responsible and could go to jail. These are just a few examples of the types of situations that we all have.

When I look at my personal life, I had my own set of high stakes situations, with divorce, family drama, and aging and sick parents. I am a more experienced poker player than I would ever like to be, personally and professionally.

Sometimes, I look back over the past 36 years and I wonder what has kept me together when I was dealing with this type of pressure, at work and in my personal life. However, I am still alive, and continuing to play high stakes poker in all aspects of my life. I am sharing with you some tips and techniques that have worked for me through the years to alleviate that heavy "weight on your shoulders" and give you some viable alternatives.

After retiring, I followed my own dreams and became a professional executive coach, and have been living my dream life. With my extensive experience and training, I continued to rely on the strategies that I learned in the corporate world on how to deal with high stakes. This was the "norm" in that world!

Recently, I had a huge client presentation that I had been preparing for, and everything had gone perfectly until the morning of the workshop. I was at the top of my game when I walked into the conference room at 8:00 to get set up and suddenly I had this sick feeling in my stomach. The realization hit me that I had left my PC at home, with my entire presentation on it, and the only thing that I had with me was a paper copy and my reference packages for the participants.

Having been in so many high stakes situations in the corporate world, this was my first "bad hand" in my own personal business. The room was filling up, the clock was ticking and the pit in my stomach was getting worse. I knew that I had to make some decisions very quickly. I was either going to have to fold or create a small miracle to ensure a positive outcome for the client and myself. I stepped outside of the conference room, took a deep breath and started thinking about the things that had worked for me in the past.

Focusing on these things gave me a sense of calmness and competence. Those few minutes outside the conference room gave me time to think and to see what I could do. I realized that I had everything I needed in my head and my heart, and the PC was just a prop. So, I summoned all the courage, strength and determination that I had and walked back into the conference room.

I began by telling everyone what had happened; I was very transparent and kicked off the workshop with high energy and got started. The workshop turned out to be outstanding and the feedback was excellent. Several people said that they really enjoyed me not using my PC, and it was refreshing to have someone actually present instead of using the computer. It proved to me that by keeping focused, being flexible, and staying positive, you can turn any high stakes scenario into a winning hand.

I have been using a "process" for all the major decisions in my life, and have followed these same steps after my divorce, when my mother was very ill, when my siblings were all sick at the same time, and during my entire corporate career. The process has continued to work for me through the years and when I don't follow it, the outcome is not always so good.

I want to share with you my simple and easy strategy that has worked for me in every area of my life when things got really difficult and challenging. If you will follow this process, you will find that you have much better outcomes for your situations. It's called the **CHECK** process, and has five easy steps.

- **CALM DOWN** – Our most common reaction is to panic when we are in a high stakes situation. This only makes the situation worse. I had to step outside the conference room before I could even begin to know what my next steps would be.
    - o You need a "change of venue", so remove yourself physically from the situation, if possible, so that you can have some time to clear your mind and to gather your thoughts. If you can't step out of the situation physically, then find a quiet corner where you can just take a moment to think.
    - o Don't forget to take a few deep breaths. I used to laugh when someone would say to "breathe", and now it's my best practice to calm me down physically and emotionally. Inhale and exhale slowly, and let that breath go all through your body. This will help with the tension and anxiety that you are feeling.

o Keep your emotions under control, or they can sabotage any new plans that you might have. No one is perfect, and going down the "shoulda, woulda, coulda" path is a waste of your precious energy. Refocus your energy on what you can do and not waste one second on what you didn't do.

- **HAVE GOALS** - Ensure that you have your true goals in sight, not what you *THINK* they should be. Put your focus on how to achieve the best outcome for everyone. My goal with my customer was to provide value to the participants of the workshop, and not on how I would be viewed in front of the client.

    o Know who your customer is. It is not YOU, so think about what your original goal was and how can you still achieve that goal. Focus on your impact and the overall outcome, not on yourself.
    o Determine what you can do to help, what new and different ideas you can discover, and how you can now put a plan in place with that goal in mind.
    o Take one more look at what you originally were planning to do and find another way to do that.

- **EXPLORE POSSIBILITIES** – You are outside your comfort zone, so explore all the possibilities, and be open for new options. What happens to all of us is when the plan doesn't go as we think it should, we "shut down". My first thought was just say, "My husband is on his way, let's just make the introductions, and he will be here with my PC by the time we are finished". As I thought about that option, I knew that it would not work. The workshop would have begun with very low energy, and the rest of the day would have been lost. I had to find another possibility to achieve my goals.

- o Be open to new possibilities, and don't hold on to your old ideas. Get creative and see what other options are out there.
- o Let go of your original plans and expectations. When we have high expectations, we are always disappointed, as the outcome never meets those expectations.
- o Be flexible, think "outside the box", and be prepared to do something out of character for you or even outrageous. Sometimes I think of someone who I admire and say to myself, "What would Susan do in this situation?" That gives me options that I might not have thought of.

- **CREATE A PLAN** – Once you have looked at the options, you can create a new plan. My new plan was to find other ways to give my presentation without the use of the visuals that were on my PC. I had to become very creative in order to provide value to my clients.

- o Know what your goals are and how you will achieve them
- o Determine what value you are delivering, and keep the focus not on you, and remember what is at stake in this situation.
- o Develop a plan of action that you can deliver with ease and confidence. These have to be your actions and you must feel comfortable in which steps you choose.

- **KEEP FOCUSED** - Remember to be authentic and keep it simple. I walked into the client and was honest and told them all what was going on. This took the pressure off me and then I could be myself.

    o Don't over think or overcomplicate the situation. Too often, we become paralyzed because we are making the solution too hard.
    o Be yourself, authentic and honest. No one is perfect and your clients, family, and friends will appreciate who you are. I read somewhere that when you are "vulnerable", that allows others to be themselves as well.

The **CHECK** system is an excellent strategy, but it's not easy to implement. The most common thing that happens, and it happened to me many times, is that self-doubt, lack of confidence, and fear come into the play. This has paralyzed me, stopped me dead in my tracks, and made my heart feel like it was going to jump out of my chest. That's what happened to me at my client's office, but I was able to put the **CHECK** strategy into play and I turned a disastrous hand into a truly winning hand. It was a *"win-win"* for everyone, the client was happy, I was happy and most of all, the participants in the workshop received huge value from our work together. What a great day!

How have I been able to overcome my own self-doubt and fear as I have faced these incredible stressful and high stakes situations? I use the **CHECK** strategy that I shared with you, then I ask myself that same question every time that I am dealt a bad hand or a situation is not what I want it to be. The answer is always the same...**IT COMES DOWN TO ME**. It's about training yourself to realize that you have the power to change any situation from negative to positive. It's up to you to find the silver lining and turn it around, but you are the only one that can change your reaction and how you choose to handle the situation.

It is about asking yourself, "What if I don't have a PC, what is the worst that can happen?", and then turning it around and saying "what if I don't have a PC, what is the best thing that can happen?" Suddenly, endless possibilities open up and you have choices that you didn't know you had before.

As you are sitting at that "Poker Game of Your Life" and the stakes get so high you can't breathe, and the knot in your stomach continues to grow, remember to ask yourself the question "what if?" in a positive way. Put yourself "**IN CHECK**", follow the process and strategies that you have learned, you will have a winning hand and you will truly become an **UNSTOPPABLE WOMAN!**

Cena Block, Mom-preneur Clarity Catalyst helps people find sanity through clear spaces, efficient systems, understanding themselves, and getting the support they need for success.

Cena is the owner of Sane Spaces, LLC, a Productivity Consulting and professional services firm that offers productivity services, training, life coaching, and motivational speaking to individuals and organizations.

As President of the Northern NJ Chapter of the National Association of Professional Organizers (NAPO), and a member of both national NAPO and the Institute for Challenging Disorganization (ICD), she regularly attends seminars, professional trainings and workshops, continually building on her expertise, services and coaching tools.

Cena's commitment is helping professional moms and Mom-Preneurs who do it all find balance, enrichment, fulfillment, and clarity while living a life they love. She's worked through the process... and she can help you find your way too.

Cena shares her life with her husband and two sons who are living daily knowing both the struggles and joys of balancing their full lives.

Sane Spaces *Slice of Sanity* eZine gives subscribers ideas and inspiration to get clear and out from under whatever is stopping them.

Contact information:
http://www.sanespaces.com
cena@sanespaces.com

Chapter 5
Getting it All Done - Prioritizing
by: Cena Block

The picture is all too familiar: *Kelly looks in her rearview mirror to see her beautiful little boy staring out the window as the world whizzes by, safely strapped into his car seat. Unexplainable tears well up in her eyes as she realizes the incredible gift of life she's helped to create, and in that moment she feels peace. But within seconds, her thoughts are aware of the traffic around her, the board agenda for the meeting beginning in 20 minutes and whether she remembered to attach it to the email reminder she sent yesterday...*

Beside her sits a bag with a change of clothes, fresh diapers, healthy snacks she's prepared the night before, his favorite books, special toys for her son and, of course her briefcase. She's driving too fast, checking her watch, and totally perturbed with the fact that the light at the corner just turned red. Her thoughts race from her colleagues at work, to her projects, to the upcoming weekend barbeque (for which she still needs to buy and prepare food).

She bounces from one thought to the next as her eyes glaze over. The light changes and she plows forward toward the babysitter's to drop off her son and start her over-packed day. She ponders her weekly schedule in her mind – placing puzzle pieces of time together in the most efficient way to get it all done by Friday, when her folks will arrive at 3:00pm to her clean, inviting home... upholding that ever-present illusion that she can and does do it all.

Is this familiar? Crazy? Overwhelming? Exhausting? Typical? If so – read on...

My guess is that you ARE unstoppable... that you tend to always be in unstoppable action, and the reason you've found this book is that you are looking for ways to find your own sense of wellness. So, to prepare to write this chapter, I did some research, hosted interviews, brainstormed and did a lot of thinking. My conundrum was how to encapsulate 44 years of life-experience, 6 years of college education, 31 years of performance experience as a musician, 21 years of applied career experiences as a performance improvement manager, and coach, 19 years of marriage, 16 years of motherhood, countless hours spent in training and certifications in related fields, and 4 years of defining my own productivity business into valuable "wellness" advice for unstoppable women like you.

For me, the secret to 'Getting It All Done' and feeling well in the process, lies in the sweet spot that exists when I'm able to balance these five essential elements:

1. Clarifying my perspective and determining whether it serves me.
2. Knowing myself and what is most important to me.
3. Finding personal motivation, repeatedly.
4. Minimizing self-driven limitations and barriers.
5. Consistently aligning my actions to make a positive contribution.

My journey to wellness while getting it all done was very similar to the earlier scene. That example well-encapsulates five minutes of a typical morning for me not too long ago. Ironically, as I look back, it was at a time in my life when I felt I was truly succeeding at the game of getting it all done. What always seemed to be missing then though, was a sense of "wellness" – harmony, balance, and vitality.

What I lived then seemed like an overwhelming rollercoaster ride made of more to do than I had energy to accomplish, yet trying unstoppably to do it ALL. My definition of getting it all done then came at a high cost. I felt deep anguish regarding the duality of my life as a professional and as a new mom, and everything suffered, from my marriage, to my happiness – and finally to my health.

Things happen for a reason, and it took all of my life experiences to gain perspective. Can two things be true at once? Can you be unstoppable, while maintaining your sense of wellness?

That always and only, depends on you. Today, my 'getting it all done while maintaining wellness' sweet spot occurs **not** when I've checked everything off my list (although I must admit, I do love that). My sense of wellness comes when I have a tangible, confident sense of accomplishment and freedom. It is when a completed project, experience, activity or interaction "feels" just right and is not compromised, negotiated, limited or tainted by internal judgment or external noise in reflection. This feeling comes when my skills and abilities have been challenged enough to feel that hum of vitality, adventure, and knowing that what I did mattered even if only in some small way.

So, this chapter is NOT another "How-To-Do-It" better, faster, or more efficiently. Rather, this chapter is written for you, Unstoppable Woman, as a guide to wellness along your own yellow brick road. Consider this chapter a set of billboards on a personal journey defining WHAT you'll do to create wellness within your unstoppability.

This chapter will help you explore your own assumptions, beliefs, values, and goals. You'll have the opportunity to look into what "getting it all done" really means to you and from where your assumptions derive. You'll have exercises to help you explore your perspectives, clarify what is important, identify what motivates you, and see what might be in your way to taking powerful actions. The actions are always and ONLY up to you!

But I warn you: reading, pondering, and thinking are fundamentally different than taking planned and intentional actions toward meeting your goals. Being an unstoppable woman and well at the same time requires you to take intentional actions repeatedly to produce certain desired results in your life.

Your likelihood for success increases with every action you take toward actualizing a wellness strategy. You've already taken the first action by purchasing this book as your first investment. The next step will be to work through the ten journal activities in this section. The key catalytic factor for personal change is when you accept accountability and take action.

I believe that most successful people take 100% accountability for everything they do and accept no excuses. So as your productivity coach, consider the time you spend reading and working through this chapter as an important investment in your journey toward getting it all done.

Each segment is designed for you to STOP and reflect first. Journaling your thoughts will allow you valuable thinking and processing time needed to gain clarity. Each segment has journaling activities, and then invites you to identify your very next step, set up support, and take action right away... that will move you powerfully forward in your life.

Getting It Done Begins With:
Defining Your Perspective

In college I took a course in which the professor spent the first three classes focusing solely upon the title of the class itself. Deeply exploring the four words that titled the class was an exercise designed to identify my own meanings about those words. This exercise helped me think differently and ultimately broadened my perspective about the messages conveyed through the words we use.

I was formally introduced to "perspectives" work through Master Certified Mentor Coach Denslow Brown, (CPO, CPO-CD, SCAC, MCC) and Founder of Coach Approach for Organizers™. She defines perspective as *a point of view or attitude...that can impact a person negatively or positively – be useful or problematic.*

With your own perspectives in mind use the following exercise to help clarify your perspective on getting it all done.

Journal Exercise 1 –
Clarifying My Perspective
Get your notebook and pen, and begin with this first exercise. Focus on the following phrase: **"Getting It All Done"**

1. If a friend asked you: "*What does getting it all done, look like to you?*" how would you answer her?
2. Take some time to journal. Record your thoughts on getting it all done.
3. Draw your Getting It All Done Vision: use pictures, maps, lists, or doodles.
4. Consider your perspective by defining this statement one segment at a time.

a. Define what "it" is in concrete terms.

b. What does "getting it done" mean to you?

c. What does "all done" mean, look like and feel like to you?

d. Does your definition of "done" differ from "getting it all done"? If so, journal about the difference between those statements.

5. Define this statement for yourself in everyday terms: What does getting it all done look and feel like daily, weekly, monthly?
   (Ex. I accomplish everything on my to do list, I am on time for meetings, I have time for me, my family, my chosen occupation.)

6. Clarify what actions you are willing to take to achieve success at Getting It All Done. (The key is being specific on what you'll do to achieve this goal.)

   a. **Daily** – *(Ex: I will do something each day for my own health and wellness. I am in communication, on time and present. I will take 10 minutes of my day to plan my tasks within the time I have available for the next day. I will prioritize what is important. I will minimize distractions to accomplish my three most important tasks.)*

   b. **Monthly** – *(Ex: I will plan my work and work my plan. I will fulfill my commitments to myself, my family, my spouse, and my community. I will hold a family meeting weekly, support my children's activities, hold them accountable for their chores, provide at least five healthy family dinners weekly)*

    c. **Yearly** - (*Ex: I will refinish the deck and paint my bedroom. I stay within my budget. I will take a family vacation. I will host two family celebrations, I will contribute 10% to charitable causes, I will attend one personal retreat.*)

7. Now shift. If the same friend asked you: "*What does 'living in wellness', look like to you?*" how would you answer?

8. Define this statement for yourself in everyday terms: What does "wellness" look and feel like daily, weekly, monthly? (*Ex. I exercise every day, I go out with my husband once per month, I have time for me, I get my hair done, I eat organic, fresh food, etc.*)

9. Take some time to journal your thoughts on wellness.
10. Draw your Wellness Vision: use pictures, maps, lists, or doodles.
11. Reflect on the statement: "I am unstoppable and well at the same time". What do you notice about your perspective? Is this perspective serving you the life you envision as well?
12. Does your perspective contribute to your sense of satisfaction?

13. How has this journal exercise shifted, changed, or deepened your perspective?

Getting It Done Includes:
Knowing Yourself and What Is Most Important

According to the great Greek philosopher Socrates, one who knows and expresses self-knowledge in an awareness of who she

is, and what she is like, tends to take more aligned actions in her life and be ultimately more content. One of the most powerful steps to knowing yourself begins with an inquiry into your values. There may be hundreds of values that one person holds as important. But some values are so primary to our being that despite changes in society, politics, and technology they will continue to be the values we uphold and abide by throughout the course of our lives. These are known as core values.

Core values are the most essential values you hold dear. They are defined as those elements that form the foundation on which you conduct

> **"Know Thyself "-**
> *Socrates*

yourself and evaluate others. Core values are NOT given to you. They are not business or personal strategies, skills nor strengths, nor cultural or universal norms. Core values are not often changed in response to conditions or other's wishes. Core values are not descriptions of the work you do, nor the strategies you employ to accomplish your mission. Rather, core values underlie your work, your interactions with others, and they are the underpinnings behind everything you do. In an ever-changing world, your core values are constant.

Journal Exercise 2 – Selecting, Prioritizing and Defining Core Values

1st. Select Your Core Values
Review the list of values below. (This list is not exhaustive, but supplies a sampling of many different values to choose.)

Acceptance	Economic security	Influence	Responsibility
Achievement	Excellence	Leadership	Risk taking
Adventure	Excitement	Learning	Routine
Authenticity	Expertise	Love	Security
Authority	Faith	Loyalty	Self expression
Autonomy	Fairness	Making a difference	Service
Balance	Fame	Productivity	Spirituality
Beauty	Freedom	Nature	Success
Belonging	Friendship	Nurturing	Tolerance
Collaboration	Happiness	Order	Tradition
Commitment	Harmony	Passion	Trust
Community	Health	Peace	Vitality
Compassion	Helping others	Personal growth	Wholeness
Contribution	Honesty	Power	Winning
Creativity	Independence	Recognition	Wisdom

1. Identify the Top 10 values that are most essential to you. Since there are values that do not appear on the list, be sure to add any value(s) you hold as core *even if it's not on the list.*

2. When you've selected your Top 10 from the list write the values here:

MY CORE VALUES	
❏	❏
❏	❏
❏	❏
❏	❏
❏	❏

2nd. *Prioritize Your Core Values*

1. Review the values chosen from the list above, and imagine that you are only permitted to have five of these values. Which five would remain?

2. *Which value would you give up to reverse your biggest mistake/hurt you've caused?* **Mark this value with a 5.**

3. *Which value would you give up to give every human being in the world enough food for life?* **Mark that value with a 4.**

4. *Which value would you give up to bring a treasured loved one back that has passed away?* **Mark that value with a 3.**

5. *Which would you give up to turn around the atrocities of 9-11?* **Mark that value with a 2.**

6. **Mark the remaining value with a 1.** This is your most basic core value.

3rd. *Define Your Top 5 Values*

1. Use the chart below as a diagram for your journal. Transfer your top 5 values to your journal. Review your list and determine which one you are LEAST satisfied with at this moment in time.

2. In your journal specifically define what it would look and feel like if you were 100% satisfied with the value that is currently out of balance in your life. Take the time to dive deep in this exercise. The more time you take NOW to

define your satisfaction, the clearer you become to defining "enough." This activity makes your essential actions clearer and more achievable.

MY TOP VALUES	PERSONAL DEFINITION (as expressed weekly, monthly, yearly and in thought and action.)
1	
2	
3	
4	
5	

Getting It All Done Includes:
Finding a Personal Sense of Motivation

Motivation is often a critical component for action to occur. Personal motivation is articulated clearly in what you choose to do or not to do. Understanding and defining your core values

> ### *Motivation*
>
> *Internally generated drive to achieve a goal or follow a particular course of action.*

may be a very motivating step by itself. Obtaining clarity around what is most important to you and whether you are in alignment with what is important, may allow the fog to clear enough for you to feel the self-propulsion necessary to take important action steps toward being well while Getting It All Done. Highly motivated people tend to focus their efforts on achieving specific goals; those who are unmotivated do not.

But where does motivation come from? Where do we find it

repeatedly? Psychologist Abraham Maslow's *Hierarchy of Needs Theory* proposed that humans are motivated in succession through our lives by five unmet needs, in ascending categories beginning with: Survival, Safety, Social-belonging, Self-Esteem, and finally Self-Actualization.

Hierarchy of Needs Theory

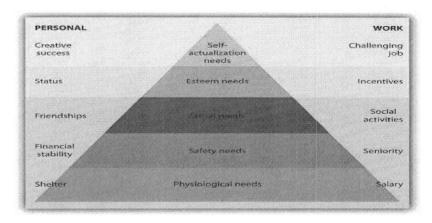

Figure 1 displays *Maslow's Hierarchy-of-Needs Theory*, and shows examples of these categories in both the personal (left-hand column) and work (right-hand column) life spheres. Contentment at the base of the pyramid is achieved when basic *physiological* needs, such as food and shelter, are met. Working up the pyramid we experience the *safety* needs of financial stability and freedom from physical harm. The *social* needs level includes the need to belong and have friends. Once *esteem* needs for self-respect and status are met, one can begin the journey toward attaining the *self-actualization* needs of reaching one's full potential and achieve creative success.

Maslow's Theory states that people seek out opportunities that satisfy their **current** needs before reaching for those in higher levels. He also claimed that people's needs changed as they progressed through each level in the hierarchy. Therefore, to ascend to higher levels, one must satisfy her needs with the underpinning level first.

Generally, the less satisfied you are with any given factor, the more motivated you are to do something about it. Conversely, the more satisfied you are with something, the less motivated you are to do something about it. When your basic (physiological and psychological) needs are satisfied, they disappear and you're able to move more purposefully toward what motivates you.

For example, if I'm feeling unfit and inactive (Cena=Dissatisfied), I'm much more motivated to exercise and avoid desert than when I'm enjoying a delicious piece of homemade chocolate cake (Cena=Satisfied). Satisfaction then is less of a motivator than dissatisfaction. Get it? When you are unhappy, you tend to be more driven to do something about it, than when you are satisfied. In order to get motivated, it's important to uncover what is NOT working for you now.

How do you do that? Focus on the negative! Now it's your turn to assess the areas in your life with which you're currently dissatisfied. Once you've figured those out, we can get on to what motivates you most!

Journal Exercise 3 – Assessing Dissatisfiers
Use the table as a model for your next journal exercise. Focus on the following statement:

"I am dissatisfied with these things in my life."

Situations, Factors, Relationships that currently dissatisfy me	NEED Category (Reference figures 1 & 2)	NEED ACTION To increase Satisfaction?	ACTIONS I can take

1. List situations, factors, and relationships that you are currently dissatisfied with down the left side of a page. Really crank-it-up, and complain! Continue listing items until you run dry of ideas.
2. Review the list and write the corresponding need category on the right column.

Journal Exercise 4 – Personal Timeline and Life Map

1. Using 5-10 pieces of plain paper, lay out a large writing

surface where you have enough room to visually draw a timeline of your life up till now. (Hint: The older you are, the more space you may need!)

2. Draw a timeline from left to right that depicts your life on earth. (DOB on left of line, Today's Date on right of line)

3. Beginning with your earliest memory, note all major life events and important milestones, experiences, opportunities and moments. (Include: schools, travels, firsts, deaths, marriage, jobs, etc.)

4. Get up and take a wiggle break, and then return to your list later.

5. Add any event you've missed:
   a. Add every job (whether paid or unpaid) to your list.
   b. Add any tragedies (loss of loved ones, illnesses, accidents, world events, etc.).
   c. Keep adding to your timeline until you are satisfied that it is an accurate visual picture of your life.

6. Review your timeline and highlight or mark the times when you've felt satisfied, driven, and most motivated.

7. What do you notice about your Timeline and Life Map? When have you been most motivated and satisfied? What is missing now in your life?

Getting It All Done Includes: Minimizing Limitations and Removing Barriers

The journey toward awareness and enlightenment is life-long. To be an unstoppable, well woman, you'll need to attain a clear understanding of where you get hung up - your limitations and barriers. Barriers are there for reasons. They protect us from danger and keep us safe. Clearly understanding what stops you will help you work toward minimizing limiting conditions and get them out of your way, so you can get onto Getting It All Done!

Highly competent, conscious, unstoppable, well women tend to:
- know what they know
- know what they are good at
- know what they don't know about their own skills and abilities

When they encounter barriers, they recognize them and work their way around them to achieve their goals.

Self-reflection offers you opportunities to identify your own strengths and gaps. Although it is a popularly held belief that to improve, you should focus on improving your weaknesses, human performance studies have shown that highly successful people focus more of their efforts on building upon their strengths and talents, and minimizing or seeking assistance with their areas of weakness.

On the journey of being well and unstoppable, let's focus on the following formula introduced in The Inner Game of Tennis, by Tim Gallwey:

Performance = Potential - Interference

Gallwey discovered this performance concept when he was coaching tennis:

"While teaching tennis one day, I realized that many of my teaching instructions were being incorporated in the student's mind as a kind of "command and control" self-dialogue that was significantly interfering with learning and performance. When I inquired into this, I found that there was a lot going on in the mind of my tennis students that was preventing true focus of attention. I then began to explore ways to focus the mind of the player on direct and non-judgmental observation of ball, body, and racquet in a way that would heighten learning, performance, and enjoyment of the process. "

Gallwey's acute observation of his tennis student's apparent internal self-dialogue and their response to the "command and control" of an expert, was the underlying cause for what he termed "interference." His hypothesis was: remove interference and performance automatically improves as the student is able to realize his/her potential because they have less interference.

Gallwey shifted his perspective, and instead of being the "expert," he focused on minimizing interference so that students could draw on their own wisdom, experiences and perceptions. Helping students to focus on awareness, caused internal interference to naturally diminish and their performance improved.

Each of us has skills, talents, abilities, and strengths. We also have areas of weakness, struggle and deficiency. Each of these areas is colored by different life experiences: country of origin, family structure, parents, siblings, our level of education, the social systems to which we've been exposed. All of this experience has had an impact on our skills, abilities and knowledge. It is important to not only know your skills, but also where you struggle.

Journal Exercise 7 –
Defining Potential & Limiting
Interference
Use this table as the format for this journal activity.

PERFORMANCE =	POTENTIAL - INTERFERENCE	
PERSONAL GOAL	*LIST STRENGTHS, EXPERTISE, ABILITIES & ATTRIBUTES.*	*LIST INTERNAL & EXTERNAL INTERFERENCE*

Although most people won't need a formula to chart and process their own self-talk, it does give a great objective viewpoint to consider when discovering and working within your barriers and limitations.

Getting It All Done & Being Well Means:
Aligning Action with Contribution

Congratulations! You've reached a milestone of self-awareness by stepping through the first four segments of Getting It All Done! Sit back, kick your feet up, and relax... your work is all done. *"WHAT??? No way!!"* says the unstoppable, well woman. *"All this potential – and no action? – But I'm not done."* She cries. *"I'm like a powder keg without a spark... Let me out there to do something!"*

71

So, what do you do now? Should you go find your favorite charity? Climb a mountain? Well, maybe, but I suggest you spend some time figuring out the best way to bring your naturally passionate, motivated, resourceful, creative, powerful, unstoppable, and well self into the world with purposeful intention and informed action.

It is innately human to seek meaningfulness in our lives. We all want the ability to know and feel that what we do matters. How do you achieve meaningfulness in what you do?

It is not easy to answer this question because the answer to such questions lies exclusively within and not outside of you. Things and situations have meaning because you attribute meaning to them. They do not have meaning by themselves but depend on your perspective, reality and system of beliefs. The same thing may have deep meaning for me but can be meaningless to you.

Meaning comes as a sum of its parts, parts dependent upon a whole. So, although much of the internal work of this chapter is now behind you, you've graduated onto the real challenge:

What is this unstoppable, well woman to do? This journal exercise will help inform your next steps.

Journal Exercise 8 –
Defining Your Essence
Please use a blank page in your journal for this activity.
1. Clarifying your "essence":
    a. Close your eyes and begin breathing deeply.

b. Journey inside your thoughts as you let go of everything that is outside of yourself.

c. Let go of your "roles": your career, your family roles, and your job responsibilities.

d. Simply focus on what is so for you – who are you in the moments that you are most satisfied.

e. What word(s) come to you when you go inside and listen to yourself?

2. Write any words down that come to mind. Think about:
   a. How the world sees you at your best.
   b. Who you are when you are most aligned, secure and content.
   c. A descriptive word consistently used by people who know you well.

3. If you have more than one word, try these questions to help:
   a. What word conveys the essence of you in the world?
   b. What word best describes you out of any of your choices?
   c. What's been you from your childhood and continues to be so?
   d. Would your friends and family agree with this?

4. Try on each of these words until you find the one that fits and feels most comfortable.

Journal Exercise 9 –
Defining Your Mission

Please use a blank page in your journal for this activity.

1. Write your "essence" on the top of a piece of paper in your journal.

My "Essence" Example Words: *Clear, Honest*

2. Craft a declarative sentence around this word or words beginning with "I am..." My "Mission" Example: *I am a clearing for other's self-expression.*
3. Let the Brainstorming begin! Brainstorm words, pictures, actions, thoughts and ideas in your journal. Brainstorming brings clarity through considering many options. And clarity purposefully moves this process forward.

Getting It All Done and Finding the Way Forward

I believe that a purposefully-driven intention and a clarified purpose does not require "how to." An informed and aligned purpose drives motivated behavior and monitors itself until it reaches its goal. The time spent clarifying, connecting, uncovering who you  are, and what is true for you internally; is a minimal investment for the exponential power conveyed when you begin to express your integrated self in action in the world.

As stated from the beginning, this chapter was never about how-to get it all done... I am a true believer that an aligned purpose, consistently motivates, measures and monitors action until the desired goal is achieved.

> "It's the action, not the fruit of the action, that's important. You have to do the right thing. It may not be in your power, may not be in your time, that there'll be any fruit. But that doesn't mean you stop doing the right thing. You may never know what results come from your action. But if you do nothing, there will be no result."
>
> — Mahatma Gandhi

Journal Exercise 10 – Creating Your Vision Board

Please use a blank page in your journal for this activity titled VISION WORDS.

1. Brainstorm words, catch phrases, pictures, symbols, and ideas in your journal.
2. Bring your Vision full-circle by searching for ideas out in the world. Images may be found in magazines, advertisements, or in pictures. Cut them out and begin collecting them.
3. Keep journaling and collecting ideas as this vision gels. Words may come at interesting times. Keep your journal with you – even at your bedside as you sleep. Dreams are powerful ways our sub-conscious helps problem-solve.
4. Create your Vision Board! Combine all your thoughts, clippings, and ideas together to create your own vision board.

Congratulations! Now what? The most worthwhile contribution

that drives a feeling of true satisfaction and "wellness" is to give of yourself. We all want meaningfulness in our lives. We all want the ability to feel as though what we do matters. It all begins with trust; take your first step and the necessary path will be revealed! Getting it all done for the unstoppable well woman means finding your own sweet spot. It will be revealed as you balance among all the treasures you bring into the world.

The unstoppable woman finds wellness by:
holding on to intention while letting go of results,
creating her purposeful future vision while honoring her past,
planning for success yet being flexible to change,
prioritizing her tasks while focusing on the future,
enjoying the present moment while anticipating what is next,
working on what matters most yet not sweating too many details,
efficiently managing her activities while being open to what comes
by,
saying no and saying yes, and doing and not doing.
The unstoppable woman finds wellness by determining what is
most important and letting the rest go.
Because it is, was and ever will be
only and always
what you do that matters....

Tamela Douglas-Bland has always had a heart and passion for helping others. Born and raised on the west-side of Chicago, IL, the second child of three girls and one boy. She is a loving wife and mother of three daughters. Her passion for helping others was clearly demonstrated as she opened a daycare center called "Lil Lullabies" and helped educate children. Being certified in massage therapy and having a strong desire to do more in the medical field, she became a medical administrator's assistance, and a nurse's assistant. Even after obtaining a class A Driver's License, Tamela found ways to be of some assistance to fellow truck drivers during the one year course of her experience. Returning to the health care field she helps senior citizens in a northwestern suburb while concurrently building her own business with the purpose of showing others how to save as-well-as make money. In her spare time she likes doing anything with her family, attending church, skating, swimming, writing poems, watching movies, traveling, and growing her business.

Firsthand experience has allowed her to understand the importance of being aware of another person's intentions and future plans in order to maintain a healthy and emotionally well relationship.

Contact information:
tamelabland@ymail.com
www.forwardmotionnow.info

Chapter 6

7 Things You Should Know
Before You Commit
by: Tamela Douglas-Bland

The thought of being in a loyal and committed relationship is very appealing to many of us. We strive to obtain the type of bond with another person that will allow us to grow as individuals, and evolve as a unit. In the search for a significant other, we experience varying degrees of issues, drama, and other undesirable elements.

Wouldn't it be great if we could somehow gauge whether or not the relationship was going to work out *before* we invested our precious time? This chapter is designed to do just that. I have compiled a list of core things that you should know before deciding to commit to the relationship. These elements aren't just for you to know, but your significant other as well. So, I invite you to share this chapter with them to see if you're both on the same page.

1. Love Yourself

Before you can expect anyone else to love you, you must first love yourself. When learning to love yourself, you learn how to please yourself and find what makes you happy. You can go places, do things, or just sit at home by yourself and not be miserable. When you can entertain yourself or treat yourself to whatever you like, you are not  dependent on someone else to make you happy, which allows you to maintain control of your own life as opposed to relying on someone else. So if and when you do allow someone else into your world that wants to make you happy, you have a compliment to your life and not a codependency on someone else's. When you truly love yourself, you set your deal breakers and let them be known. A deal breaker is an action that occurs causing the relationship to end beyond a shadow of a doubt. For instance: cheating, lying, abuse, etc. When you truly love yourself you also set a standard of the way you want to be treated.

To allow someone to treat you in a way that is beneath the standards you have set is no one's fault but your own and it will only bring you heartache. I'm not saying that you have to be conceited. In my opinion, someone who is humble is more attractive. What I am asking you to please remember is that you are a beautiful gift from God; do not allow anyone to treat you as anything less. I would like to share an excerpt from a poem I wrote in 2005 called "God's gift":

> *...Loving and supportive doing whatever it takes,*
> *someone else will benefit from your mistakes.*
> *Now I don't need a man to show me my worth.*
> *It's been instilled in me since the day of my birth.*
> *See I "choose" to have a man to share my life with,*
> *because there's just so much joy and love I want to give.*
> *But it has to be someone who feels the same,*
> *"a good woman should be cherished not used in vain..."*

2. Know What You Want (Goals)

Knowing what you want should inspire you to set goals for your life. It is never too late to set goals, focus on them, and take the proper steps to achieve them. I like to believe that goals are your dreams waiting to become your reality. So don't let anyone or anything distract you and by all means never let anyone steal them. Knowing what you want is the first step in getting what you want, but sometimes wanting something is not enough. One could say, "When I grow up I want to get a job, get a house, get married, have children, and send them to college." There are too many unknowns. What type of job? What type of house and where will it be located? What type of person will you marry? How many children, and how will you send them to college? It's important to be specific. Let's respectively focus on getting married. Now this chapter is not the "10 Commandments" to marriage or general relationships, but when seeking a significant other you need to know what it is you want. I am not just referring to the physical beauty, but the inner beauty as well.

While we all know, most times it's the outward beauty that initially attracts us, when your mate's hair begins to thin, can they make you laugh? When their six-pack becomes a keg, will you have someone who can comfort you? As gravity takes its toll or as the gray hairs begin to surface, do you have someone who is supportive? Or do you have someone who is so shallow that they leave as your body goes through the same aforementioned changes?

Know what it is you want in a mate and find it. Do not try to change someone to make them what you want. Do not fall in love with the *idea* of someone hoping things will turn out for the best. Take a moment now to choose the top 10 things that you want in a relationship from the list on the following page:

Non Abusive	Mono-gamous	Great Communicator	Humble	Supportive
Trust-worthy	Non-Judgmental	Sexual Compatibility	Honest	Protector
Involved Parent	Healthy/Fit	Financially Stable	Great Provider	Goal Oriented
Accom-plished In Career	Spiritual	Great Listener	Underst anding	Romantic
Attentive	Secure with Themselves	Respectful	Sense of Humor	Family Oriented

List them here:

_____

_____

Now, have your potential significant other complete the same exercise. Once the two of have done that, compare your top values to see if they're in alignment. This is a great way to start a conversation about the direction of the relationship.

3. See Things As They Really Are

See things as they really are not as you want them to be. When contemplating commitment, you have to be realistic with yourself. If you're dating a truck driver that doesn't spend time with you when not on the road, do not tell yourself he's just really busy. If you repeatedly catch your mate in a lie, do not make excuses for them; see them for what they are "a liar". If you are intimate with someone before establishing a relationship, do not automatically assume you have a relationship after the act of intimacy. If you're dating someone who always comes to visit you and never takes you home with them, they may be hiding more than dirty laundry (no pun intended).

 Allow me to share a personal experience, I was dating a man who always came to visit me but when I asked to see his place, he told me the mere fact that I asked to see his place made him feel like I did not trust him. After I found out where he lived I stopped by for a surprise visit. The surprise was on me when another woman answered the door stating she was his girlfriend of eight years, and that I was not the first woman he cheated on her with. During the entire period of my visit he stayed locked in the bedroom, would not come out nor answer any phone calls from me while I was there. The girlfriend asked me if he had begun to ask me for money. When I told her no he had actually been buying meals for me and my children, she informed me that she had given him the money when he told her there was a mission to feed needy families. She knew which restaurants the meals I had had come from without me telling her. Needless to say my relationship ended that day.

When you see a situation for what it is, don't be afraid to act on it or walk away from it. Love yourself enough to know that you deserve nothing short of what you give. If you give your all to someone then you deserve that someone's all in return. When you are faithful to someone, you deserve that someone's faithfulness in return not just their loyalty, there is a difference. In the 2004 movie Ray, written by James L. White, Ray Charles was not faithful to his wife but he was loyal to her, making it clear to his mistress that he would never leave his wife. While this may be acceptable to some, to others it is a deal breaker.

4. The Art of Communication

Learning to communicate does not have to be difficult, but lack thereof can be cumbersome. If your mate asks if you like ice cream, you may say, "yes." When you are offered vanilla, you may say, "I only like chocolate." When you are offered chocolate in a bowl, you may say, "I only like it on a cone." When offered chocolate ice cream on a plain cone, you may say, "I only like sugar cones," and he may then say, with eyebrows raised, "Look here, how about you get your own ice cream!"

Sometimes it can be as simple as giving all of the information at one time/expressing yourself completely. The statement, "I want to be comforted", to most people means I want to be held or I need a hug. Someone who grew up in a home that was not very touchy-feely may interpret the statement to mean, "I need someone to talk to," and I am not saying that that is wrong because that may be the way that person needs to be comforted. What I am saying is you need to communicate exactly what you want your mate to know.

Sometimes communication may be as simple as listening or receiving the message in whatever way you are capable, be it in a written format or through sign language. The dictionary defines communication as "an exchange of information or opinions." The keyword here is exchange, give, and receive. But if there is no listening involved, true communication has not occurred. Consider the communication gaps in the following chart:

What Is Said	What Women Mean	What Men Mean
I don't have anything to wear	I want to go shopping	I need to do laundry
I'm hungry	Let's go out to eat	Go cook us something to eat

5. Finances

Establish your own finances. Long gone are the days where men are looking for women to take care of. In this day and age there are some men who are looking for a woman to take care of them. I say to that, "To each his own." I do not judge anyone, but one thing that needs serious consideration is your future. Let's just say you find that one rare soul that wants to  take care of you for the rest of your life. He does not want you to work, but rather take care of home and the children. What happens if his life comes to an unexpected end? Will you be able to maintain your home, yourself, and your children? Or what if you find that it was all just a mind game, a method of control to keep you under his thumb? If you don't have your own income, you have to ask for money, which pretty much keeps your mate in control of your every move. So when he's angry about any little thing and decides he doesn't want you to go anywhere, you won't go anywhere until he decides you will. When you establish your own finances, no one can tell you when or where to go or what to do. You decide if you deserve a new outfit, to have your hair or nails done, or to get a massage.

It's also important to know how they manage their money. If you're someone who likes to save money, invest, and pay bills on time, and he likes to spend his money on clothes, car accessories, and video games without any regard for saving, this may cause a conflict should you decide to further the relationship.

How will you manage the funds together? Will you have separate accounts or joint accounts? What values about money will you teach your children? How does your credit score compare to his? Having your own discretionary income provides a "safety net" if your values about money don't gel.

6. Religious Preferences

When it comes to religious preferences you may want to select someone who shares the same religious beliefs as you. This is not to say that different beliefs cannot coexist under the same roof, but let's say you choose someone who practices the Muslim religion, you may want to have a separate set of kitchenware to prepare their meals. Someone who practices under the Jewish law may want kosher dishes, utensils and food. On the other hand, you may pair up with someone who does not know how to coexist, and is bent on condemning you if you do not convert.

Having different religious backgrounds plays a heavy role in how you view the world. It also weighs heavily in how you raise your children. Which religion will your child have? Perhaps you want to let the child select his or her own religion when they're old enough to do so, and he wants to raise the child in his faith from the beginning. How does practicing two different religions affect your relationship with your families? In any case know what you want, make a decision do not waiver.

7. Be Able To Give As Well As Receive

Relationships are about giving as well as taking. My mom once said, "Don't be a graveyard, it only takes, takes, takes and never gives anything." Being able to give as well as receive is not just referring to materialism. Bring something to the table in your relationship. Everyone wants their mate to be a great provider and take very good care of them, but you also need to take very good care of your mate. While making your own money, keeping a clean house, doing laundry, paying bills, and preparing meals, just as you would if you were living alone, know that there is more. You also need to know how to listen well, be supportive, encouraging, uplifting, protective, and comforting (yes ladies, men do need comforting). Think about all the things you have to offer and don't be afraid to share them with your mate. So don't be a graveyard and do not commit to a graveyard. Give-and-take, it's a two way street.

Many women can easily produce a long list of things that they want from their significant other. They may say they want companionship, loyalty, financial responsibility, and passion. But when asking those same women what they have to ***offer*** a relationship, there's usually a long pause before they deliver a list that's less than half of the things they listed before. It's not just about what you want **from** them, but also what you have to **give** them.

No relationship is easy breezy. In fact, I would question the growth of any relationship that didn't endure some type of challenge along the way. But utilizing these 7 things will place you on an excellent track to a healthy, and loving relationship. Unstoppable women deserve it!

Dr. Evelyn Hudson has a special ministry for individuals who suffer from rejection, emotional trauma, broken marriages, divorce, separation, and rape, emotional and physical abuse.

Dr. Hudson is a member of the Board of Education for Kansas City Kansas Public Schools, a recent board member of the KCK Chamber of Commerce, and an immediate pass Chair-person of the Kansas Black Chamber of Commerce. She has volunteered for the Wyandotte County United Way, the Keeler Women's Center, Leadership 2000 and the Unified Government of Wyandotte County.

Dr. Hudson serves as Pastor of the Memorial Christian Outreach Church, under the Leadership of Apostle Larry and Pastor Olivia Aiken of the Memorial Missionary Baptist Church International. Dr. Hudson is currently employed by City Vision Inc, as Director of Property Mgmt & Leasing.

Her education includes a Bachelor of Arts – Human Resources Management - Mid America Nazarene College, a Masters Degree - Theology - Faith Bible College, and a Doctorate Degree - Scriptural Psychology - Faith Bible College

Training: Bank of America Neighborhood Excellence Leadership Training, Civic Leadership Training Council, Inc., Success Measures Training, Kansas Leadership Community Initiative, Contemporary Consultant/ Master Facilitation Training

Dr. Hudson has received the 2001 Distinguished Leader Award, and the 2002 Black Distinguish Women Award in Kansas City, Kansas.

Contact information:
evelyn@cvmkck.org
ehudson1@kc.rr.com
www.EvelynHudsonEnterprises.com

Chapter 7

The Storm Has Passed –
Picking Up the Pieces
by: Dr. Evelyn Hudson

On Sunday, May 22, 2011, an EF-5 tornado hit the city of Joplin, Mo., leaving an estimated 151 people dead. The Joplin tornado is the deadliest single tornado since modern record keeping began in 1950 and is ranked as the 7th deadliest in U.S. history. Eight-thousand housing units were destroyed by the killer tornado. That total includes homes, apartment buildings and nursing homes in the six-mile path.

Ashford Portal Blog

After observing the devastation from the Joplin tornado on television, I had an opportunity to personally go with a friend, whose hometown was Joplin to offer help to some of the families who had just lost everything they had. What gripped my heart the most was when I drove through the neighborhoods. There were no homes, just piles of what looked like trash for blocks and blocks. Many of the people in the city had to face the storm whether they wanted to or not. After experiencing the storm, they had to figure out a way to survive.

Storms happen in our lives just like this tornado. Our lives are disturbed and disrupted. Our confidence is shaken and fear takes over. The loss and tragedy in our lives cause extreme emotional pain and suffering. The stress and anxiety of how to cope and what to do next is overwhelming. We must have courage and face the storms in our lives and have the guts to live a full life after the storm is over.

The storms of divorce, death, losing a home or job are all devastating events that may happen in life. It looks and feels like you cannot make it. But you can pick up the pieces of your life and move forward. These challenging circumstances often include financial devastation, relationship catastrophe, and self esteem destruction. Just remember you are not alone. Note the following information. It represents thousands of Americans who have been in a crisis situation, or presently experiencing a crises in their lives.

Divorce Statistics in America for Marriage

Marriage	Divorce statistics (in percent)
First Marriage	45% to 50% marriages end in divorce
Second Marriage	60% to 67% marriages end in divorce
Third Marriage	70% to 73% marriages end in divorce

Source: Jennifer Baker, Forest Institute of Professional Psychology, Springfield

Divorce continues to remain as painful as a death or a loss in the family. Even with the devastation of divorce with its effect on family members of both sides, you can survive. The economy in America has affected all of lives. Many have experienced loss one way or another. Please notice the information below:

- 2010 was a record-setting year for foreclosure filings in the U.S., with almost 2.9 million properties being foreclosed nationwide. But more than half of those filings happened in California, Florida, Arizona, Illinois, or Michigan.

- According to the Bureau of Labor Statistics US Department of Labor News Release, dated October 2011, the number of unemployed persons, at 14.0 million, was essentially unchanged in September, of this year and the unemployment rate was 9.1 percent. Since April, the rate has held in a narrow range from 9.0 to 9.2. Among the major worker groups, the unemployment rates for adult men (8.8 percent), adult women (8.1 percent), teenagers (24.6 percent), whites (8.0 percent), blacks (16.0 percent), and Hispanics (11.3 percent) showed little or no change in September.

What should you do? How do you take nothing and start over? How do you pull yourself up by the bootstraps when you have no boots? Take the following steps to move from where you are today toward your better tomorrow:

Step 1: Face the Fears

Life comes with many fears. The fear of being alone, fear of failure, fear of being broke, fear of losing the house, fear of losing a job, fear the children will not understand and blame you, the fear of losing friends and the fear of rejection to name a few. Even though you feel the grip of fear you must talk to yourself and say, "I will not fear." You must say to yourself you will NOT fear every day. When you walk away from fear you walk into faith that always says "you can make it". Feel free to tell yourself I can do this, and whatever it is YOU will do it.

So where do you start?

a. **Focus.** "Get Your Groove Back!" Who are *you* and what do *you* want to accomplish? You must start a new chapter in your life. It will require focus. (Read the

book called , "*The Power of Focus*" by *Jack Canfield*.)
Follow the instructions.

b. **Set goals with timelines and completion dates**.
Career goals, financial goals, household goals, cooking
goals, health goals and goals for your young children.

c. **Do what you do not want to do first.** Do what you
dread to do first instead of last. Then you get
everything else done fast. If it is seeking to get
financial help after a foreclosure or separating and
distributing clothes after the death of a love one or even
identifying a new place to live that is cheaper that you
can afford. **Do that task first.** Stop procrastinating.
Do it first, get it over with so you move on.

d. **Associate yourself with successful women**. You are
going to be amazed at how many successful women
have survived a life crisis such as divorce or death of a
loved one and have lived life victoriously. Many have
started businesses, wrote books, and became executives
in large organizations. They have purchased houses,
cars and rental property. The sky is the limit!!! I
encourage you to aim high for the sky!

e. **Go where you have never gone before**. Take a
journey that feels uncomfortable or risky. Visit or
possibly join organizations like your local Chamber of
Commerce, Rotary Club or any other community
organization that you may be interested in, especially if
it helps those less fortunate than yourself. It will take
your mind off of your pain and cause you to learn new
things about your city, county and community while
you meet new people.

Step 2: Heal Your Attitude.

This is the key to your success. The emotional pain from a divorce and traumatic experiences in life must be dealt with immediately. A good counselor will help you navigate through the different emotions that you may be experiencing. Emotions such as anger, guilt, shame, hopelessness, and fear are difficult to manage alone, but a positive attitude has many benefits. According to **Remez Sasson' in The Power of Positive Attitude,** "A positive attitude helps one to cope more easily with the daily affairs of life. It brings optimism into your life, and makes it easier to avoid worry and negative thinking."

If you adopt it as a way of life, it will bring constructive changes into your life, and makes one happier, brighter and more successful. With a positive attitude you see the bright side of life, become optimistic and **expect** the best to happen. It is certainly a state of mind that is well worth developing and strengthening. Your new attitude is FREE for the taking and is a benefit to the emotional fabric of your being. Establish an "I can do it" attitude. You may have to change your present thought processing, but it will be well worth it.

How can one heal emotional scaring?

1. **Forgive them**.... Whoever hurt you, whatever they did, for however long it happened, forgive them. According to Katherine Piderman, Ph.D., a Chaplain at the Mayo Clinic in Rochechester, Minnesota, "There are benefits in forgiving someone who hurt you. Letting go of grudges and bitterness makes way for compassion, kindness and peace. Forgiveness can lead to: Healthier relationships, greater spiritual and psychological well-being, less stress and hostility, lower blood pressure, fewer symptoms of depression, anxiety and chronic pain,

lower risk of alcohol and substance abuse." Forgiveness doesn't mean that other person's responsibility for hurting you doesn't exist, and it doesn't minimize or justify the wrong-doing. Forgive the person without excusing the act. Forgiveness brings a kind of peace that helps you go on with life. Don't forget to forgive yourself too!

2. **No more pity parties** .... Put the booze away, and no more smokes of any kind. Please do yourself a favor and take a straight shot of honesty. Inventory your situation and realize that pity parties are not productive. Pity parties can hinder the accomplishments of today. Deal with your pain, admit the truth, do the work that your counselor suggests, and turn your pity parties into **"destiny rides."** Destiny is calling for you, so put away the Kleenex box and get busy planning and activating your future!

3. **Eliminate Toxic Waste**...... One of the worst things that can happen to our natural environment is toxic waste. These unwanted deadly chemicals, (often from nuclear waste) could end up in our in our food and water if they are not eliminated from systems that could contaminate our natural resources. Just as toxic waste needs to be eliminated from environmental systems that could affect our health, so does negative toxic voices that hinder us from moving forward. These are people who tolerate you instead of celebrating you, and they say they are with you but often cause pain from their words or their deeds. These could be loved ones that you don't need to be in your ear at this season in your life. While you are making changes in your life, eliminate or decrease the amount of times these people

speak to you. Allow voices of hope that challenge you to move forward and encourage you to be the best you can be without destroying your already weak and/or fragile self esteem.

Picking up the pieces after the death of loved one can be extremely difficult to say the least. Death is so final, so eternal, so absolute. There are no more opportunities to communicate. No more opportunities to hug or look into the eyes of the loved one. Just like divorce, you must deal with the emotional ride of death, guilt, blame, anger, fear and more when a loved one dies. The good news is that it is very normal to experience these emotions after their death. How do you cope with death? Just remember this: Everybody grieves differently. Some may grieve without tears, while others become water fountains of tears, either way just be patient with yourself while you grieve. Allow yourself the all the time you need to grieve. Cry if you must, but continue to keep you busy.

Here are several things you can do to help you through that journey:

#1 Journal. Write your feelings down, get them out of your head and submit your thoughts to paper. You will be surprised at the pressure it takes off of your mind.
#2 Read a book that you enjoy. This will help you think about other things while you are alone.
 # Take time to exercise. Take a Zumba class or just walk. Move around, and don't just sit without doing anything. Keep moving forward.
 # Call on your friends and schedule times for lunch, dinner, or shopping even when you don't really feel like it.

You will enjoy the experience and soon find that you are gradually healing from the pain of death.

I have shared this chapter with you from the voice of experience. I want to encourage you to move from a Victim Mentality to Victor Mentality. It's all about *you*. The ball is in your court. What will you do with the ball? Unstoppable women will surely score!

 South African author, Debbie De Jager, is not only a wife and mother, but also a Certified John Maxwell Coach, Teacher and Speaker. Instead of being career-driven, Debbie is a passion-driven woman. She has an unquenchable desire to see people's lives changed as they discover their purpose in life.

Debbie worked for one of the major corporate banks in South Africa for 15 years. During this time she received 4 company awards: a Maverick Award; two Service Awards; and a Segment Innovation Award. Although being a leader to subordinates is challenging, she successfully became a leader in the organisation to almost 300 of her peers – achieving "a higher level of leadership". For this leadership role, she ultimately received a National Award in South Africa in 2010.

In order to become a woman of value, Debbie believes she has to add value to every person in her life. She teaches that strong business leaders should also have strong personal lives. Deeply joyful people are people with healthy family lives, who work in their strength zones and therefore enjoy what they do. By teaching these principles and rules, Debbie would like to add value to your life. She adds, "Thank you to Dr. Bruce H. Wilkinson and Dr. John C. Maxwell for mentoring and changing my life with your teachings!"

Contact information:
Number: +27 (0) 79 498 4875
debbiedejager@johnmaxwellgroup.com
www.johnmaxwellgroup.com/debbiedejager/
www.facebook.com/DebbieDeJager.JohnMaxwellGroup
https://twitter.com/#!/DebbieDeJager

Chapter 8

Becoming a Woman of Value
by: Debbie De Jager

Every woman grows up in a different home with varying expectations of what her future will be like. Every dream of every young woman is formed by what she experienced as a child. She might dream of one day having an attractive 'prince' sweeping her off her feet and living happily ever after. Some women dream of becoming a mother and holding her baby for the first time while others dream of having an extraordinary career and making lots of money. But undoubtedly, there are women amongst us who grow up without dreams, without aspirations. It doesn't matter whether you had childhood dreams or not, I would like to invite you to join me on a journey to become a woman of value. You have the ability within you to make a difference. You have an opportunity to leave a legacy and your life can make an everlasting impact on the people around you. Your life counts!

As we journey through three different relationships in our lives: wife, mother, and career woman, I would like to encourage you to do some introspection – look deep into your heart and examine your motives and your reason for living. So let's get to it!

Becoming a Wife of Value
Falling in love and experiencing the love of another human being is without a doubt one of the greatest blessings bestowed on mankind. In the beginning of a marriage, it's so easy to love your husband. You don't want to do anything without him and you don't want to be without him for a single minute. This reaction to love or to being in love is universal. No person who is utterly in love has to motivate themselves to spend time with the other

person. If they did, they would not truly be in love. Actually, when you first fall in love, you have to control yourself not to drown your loved one with gifts and love notes (or nowadays emails and text messages). You spend hours on the phone and hanging up is always challenging – the sound of your loved one's voice in your ear is the sweetest thing on earth. All of these feelings and reactions to love are normal. But something happens to our relationships when we get married. Somehow, with time, the magic fades. We become used to this person with whom we vowed to spend forever. We start taking each other for granted. In the beginning of the relationship we were so careful not to hurt each other, but somewhere along the way our focus shifts to ourselves and how we don't want to be hurt by our spouse. After years of marriage you might even have thoughts that your husband doesn't love you anymore. If the negative thoughts continue for too long, you will find yourself in a place where you just want to "give up." I would like to share with you two steps you can take TODAY to change the direction of your marriage. I started practicing these things in my marriage and the result was, we fell in love all over again. It can happen for you too.

> "Fighting for your marriage" means to wrestle against your own desire to give up, in order to stay committed. Love unconditionally and forgive quickly and completely. If you don't forgive, you will lose your love.
>
> *- Debbie De Jager -*

1. **Forgive your husband completely for past hurts.** Easier said than done! However, <u>not</u> forgiving your spouse for past hurts

builds a wall around your heart, and as time goes on you will discover that you have taken your heart (which once belonged to your husband), back. Unforgiveness destroys marriages. We might think that it was the last argument which destroyed it, but that's not true. If we dig deeper we will find a trail of unforgiveness running through our lives suffocating our love and affection for each other. When I decided to forgive my husband completely, I was set free from an emotional bondage. The freedom I experienced when I said "I forgive you" changed my life! You see, unforgiveness keeps the hurt or betrayed person captive – not the perpetrator – and forgiveness sets the one who forgives free. If the person you forgive is your spouse, the dynamics of your act of forgiveness can make him attractive to you once again. You soon realise that as in the beginning of your love, where you could not find any fault with your man, you are once again able to look past his mistakes and see him as the man you want to spend the rest of your life with. The truth is that we all make mistakes and I have found myself several times standing before my husband asking for forgiveness. In complete honesty, I thank the Lord that my husband has never given up on me!

One of my mentors explained forgiveness for your spouse in a way that changed my life. He said that for weeks he thought about the worst thing his wife could ever do to him. The obvious biggest hurt would be if his wife would allow another man into her life. She never did this, but he was struggling with the idea of forgiving his wife if she ever would hurt him like that. After days of thinking about this, he went to his wife and said: "My love, I had been thinking of the worst thing you could ever do to me and whether I would be able to forgive you for it. Today I would like to tell you that nothing will ever hurt me more than to find you in the arms of another man. I would be heartbroken to the point that no words could explain my pain. But today I make a promise to you. Should you ever be unfaithful to me, I will take time to get over the hurt, but I will forgive you completely. And once I've forgiven you, I will give my heart back to you unconditionally, whether you intend to hurt it again or not."

You see, dear woman, marriage is different than any other relationship we will ever have on this planet we call home. When you make your vows, it should be forever (provided your life is not being threatened) and nothing should be able to make you break your vows.

2. Another way to open your heart to love your husband again, and to win back his heart is to **recall the early days of your love and repeat what you did back then.** I took our love letters and read them over and over again; spent hours remembering our honeymoon and the love we felt for each other when our love was new. I then made a decision to take the children to my folks' house at least once a month for a sleepover so that we could have a date night. At first the idea was new to my husband and because we hadn't done the dating thing in a while, it was kind of uncomfortable, but having dinner together and going to the movies once a month changed our lives. We started talking again. We started spending time alone and apart from the children. We started working on our marriage. Before long, once a month was not enough and in every situation I was on the lookout for ways I could add value to my husband's life.

Marriage is a relationship that demands 100%, not 50/50. Answer the questions below to find out what value you currently add to your marriage. Make a decision today to increase your score with every passing day.

~Add the total from each column and place in the corresponding subtotal box. Then add the subtotals for your grand total score~

I am a Valuable Wife	Strongly Disagree - Strongly Agree									
I do not let unforgiveness fester in my heart against my husband.	1	2	3	4	5	6	7	8	9	10
I think of ways to improve our relationship on a daily basis.	1	2	3	4	5	6	7	8	9	10
Loving my husband is high on my priority list, and I am more in love with my husband today than when we first got married.	1	2	3	4	5	6	7	8	9	10
My husband's dreams and aspirations are important to me.	1	2	3	4	5	6	7	8	9	10
Spending time together as a couple is extremely important to us.	1	2	3	4	5	6	7	8	9	10
I make it easy for my husband to love me.	1	2	3	4	5	6	7	8	9	10
I honour my wedding vows and believe in "'til death do us part". Loyalty is a high value in our marriage.	1	2	3	4	5	6	7	8	9	10
Becoming a better wife, adds value to my own life.	1	2	3	4	5	6	7	8	9	10
I consciously look for ways to add value to my husband's life.	1	2	3	4	5	6	7	8	9	10
I highly respect my husband and he knows it.	1	2	3	4	5	6	7	8	9	10
Subtotal										

Grand Total

Rating

10-49	Don't give up on your marriage! You can add so much value to your husband and your marriage! You might want to consider marriage counseling.
50-79	You are already adding value to your marriage in more ways than one. Focus on your lowest scores and put your heart into adding value in these areas as well.
80-100	Your husband is a lucky guy! You are indeed a valuable wife!

Does your score reflect the value you've been adding to your marriage? Would you like to increase the value you add to your spouse and ultimately become a more valuable wife? Take all the areas in which you have scored 6 or less and start thinking about what you can do to increase the value you add in these areas of your marriage.

Becoming a Mother of Value

When I look at my children, I must admit that I think they are the most beautiful children on earth - my son with his sincere eyes and long black eyelashes, and my daughter with her beautiful smile and small glasses - they are the centre of my life. I cannot imagine my life without them. I don't want anything or anyone to hurt them. Yet, I cannot keep them from getting hurt. I cannot keep other children or teachers from humiliating or hurting my children's feelings because he's short or because she can't see well. The only thing I can do is to prepare my children for life. Prepare them to overcome obstacles in life and teach them how to deal with disappointment. Professionally, most of us have an idea of where we would like to go in terms of our careers. How much money would I like to earn? What level of seniority we would I to reach? Yet, when it comes to our children, we tend to think from day to day, trying to keep them busy and out of our way, so that we can reach our dreams. Before we continue, answer the following questions about your relationship with your child or children.

I am a Valuable Mother	Strongly Disagree - Strongly Agree									
As a mother I have a definite plan to raise my children as responsible adults, who will make good decisions and choose well.	1	2	3	4	5	6	7	8	9	10
My children experience my unconditional love on a daily basis.	1	2	3	4	5	6	7	8	9	10
When my children make mistakes or disappoint me, I forgive them quickly and they know that they will never do anything to disqualify them of my love.	1	2	3	4	5	6	7	8	9	10
My children have set boundaries in our home and they are disciplined in a healthy manner.	1	2	3	4	5	6	7	8	9	10
Spending quality time with my children is a responsibility I take very seriously.	1	2	3	4	5	6	7	8	9	10
I teach my children to love other people.	1	2	3	4	5	6	7	8	9	10
I teach my children to share and be grateful.	1	2	3	4	5	6	7	8	9	10
I allow my children to make decisions and then teach them to take responsibility for their choices and actions.	1	2	3	4	5	6	7	8	9	10
I consciously look for ways to add value to my children's lives (other than financially).	1	2	3	4	5	6	7	8	9	10
I have a strong desire to raise leaders who will stand out and make a positive difference in this world.	1	2	3	4	5	6	7	8	9	10
Subtotal										

Grand Total

Rating

103

10-49	As a mother who wants the best for her children, be mindful of the manner in which you raise them. You only have one opportunity at raising your children. Decide today to give it your all!
50-79	You have a loving home. Focus on your lowest scores and put your heart into adding value in these areas as well.
80-100	Your children are blessed to call you "mommy"! You are a valuable mother!

Looking at your total score above, what would you say is the value you are adding to your child's life? Are you raising a leader or a loser? Does your child have a positive attitude and self-image? Are you ashamed to visit friends or family because of how your children behave? I believe that children need three things in abundance from us as parents.

1. **LOVE.** Your child needs to know that he will never be rejected by you and that he is the most precious gift ever given to you. Your child should be used to your hugs and kisses and should be able to show affection as well. In our home, we must say "I love you" a hundred times a day, but it never

> *The best gift you can give your child is a happy marriage.*

   loses its meaning. While my children are playing, my three year old daughter will all of a sudden turn around and say to her brother: "I love you, Arno!" He will immediately respond with an "I love you too, sis." But another "love" that my children should know about, is that I love their father. My children should hear me telling my husband regularly that I love him. A child's security grows significantly when his parents love each other.

2. **ATTENTION.** Attention deprived children will do anything for attention from anyone. Not giving your child the right attention makes him or her vulnerable. I strongly believe that

naughty uncontrollable children are, in most cases, a result of busy parents who are keeping their children busy, so that they (the parents) can continue with their lives uninterrupted. Giving children quality attention, takes time and commitment from parents. If your mission in life was to have children, raise them and send them to school so that the school system could teach

> "Lack of discipline leads to frustration and self-loathing."
>
> *- Marie Chapian -*

them, you have missed the point. Your children should be taught the most valuable lessons from you. Teach them values. Teach them about being unselfish, about sharing, about caring for others. Teach your child about being a good sport. Teach them how to handle the disappointment of losing. Teach your child how to reach their potential and that they can dream and become great people. Teach your child to love people and that people are more important than worldly possessions. But teaching these things will be difficult if it's not part of who you are as a parent. If we want to raise leaders and responsible adults, we have to do introspection of our own values and beliefs on a daily basis.

I think we could all agree that raising children is no child's play. John C. Maxwell's (acclaimed author and leadership expert) father paid him to read leadership books. He knew that investing in his son's future and making sure his child knew how to work with people would impact his future. Make good decisions today regarding the way you raise your children. It will be too late once they leave your home.

3. **DISCIPLINE.** Discipline has become a "forever threat without action" in most homes. Because children are not disciplined in a healthy manner, we lose control and live with frustrated children. I strongly believe in DISCIPLINE used in conjunctions with LOVE and ATTENTION. When a child is disciplined for wrong doings, he learns that there are consequences for wrong behaviour. I have to add value to my child's life in the area of discipline, if I want to raise responsible adults. At the same token, once disciplined, I must not hold grudges against my child for his wrong behaviour. I will not let my child beg for my forgiveness. I will not humiliate my child by telling others about his failures. I will only uplift and praise my child in public. A disciplined and well-mannered child is a pleasure to all. And best of all – you'll never struggle to find babysitters for date-nights!

Becoming a Career Woman of Value
Lastly, let us examine how we can become more valuable career women. The first question I would like you to ask yourself is, "Am I career-driven or passion-driven?"

This question holds the answer to whether you will wake up before the alarm clock goes off and sing in the car on the way to work or if you continue to hit the 'snooze' button, dreading the rest of the day. You see, if you are career-driven, your life will revolve around the next increase, the next promotion, or your annual bonus. If you are passion-driven, the saying: "If you enjoy what you do, you will never work a day in your life" will resonate with you through and through. So how can you change your attitude or become passionate about your career if you don't enjoy your job? Change your focus. Let me explain.

At the age of twenty-one, I started as a Girl Friday (junior secretary) at one of South Africa's major banks. At that stage, I had no ambition of becoming an Executive Assistant. I was just happy to have a job and tried to do it to the best of my ability. However, in my last six years at the bank, I became a woman who added value to the bank, my colleagues, and my career. How did I do it? I decided to change my focus from my own career to that of my peers. I made a conscious decision to value people and become a valuable person to them on a daily basis. That is when I started the PA (Personal Assistants) Forum. I was hoping that forty PAs would join the Forum when I first emailed the invitation, but to my surprise the Forum grew to almost three hundred PAs in four years. I was not only the founding member and chairperson of the Forum, but I became a natural leader to the PAs. What I learned through my experience at the bank and the PA Forum was that anyone who adds value to people, become more valuable themselves.

If you can change your focus at the office from what you can get to what you can give, you will have people following you and adding value to your life in no time! Because of what I learned from the other PAs on the PA Forum, I became a better PA.

No one person can be successful on their own. If you decide to start adding value to your colleagues on an on-going basis, you will be astounded at the results. Before long you will be getting up before the alarm goes off and you will be singing on your way to work. You will be getting the next increase and bonus, even though you would do your work for free. Let's see how valuable you are in your career.

"Being valuable is directly linked to the amount of value you add to others."

- Debbie De Jager -

107

I am a Valuable Career Woman	Strongly Disagree - Strongly Agree									
My focus is not as much on my career as it is on that of my colleagues.	1	2	3	4	5	6	7	8	9	10
I consciously look for ways to add value to my leaders at the office.	1	2	3	4	5	6	7	8	9	10
I consciously look for ways to add value to my peers and co-workers at the office.	1	2	3	4	5	6	7	8	9	10
I consciously look for ways to add value to my subordinates at the office.	1	2	3	4	5	6	7	8	9	10
I am appreciative and show my appreciation to the cleaning staff at the office.	1	2	3	4	5	6	7	8	9	10
I take pride in delivering work of high quality and standard.	1	2	3	4	5	6	7	8	9	10
I am forever a student and do not compete with colleagues, but feel I can learn from them.	1	2	3	4	5	6	7	8	9	10
I have a serving (not a slave) attitude and my colleagues on all levels are comfortable to ask for my assistance.	1	2	3	4	5	6	7	8	9	10
I value people more than things.	1	2	3	4	5	6	7	8	9	10
I am passion-driven.	1	2	3	4	5	6	7	8	9	10
Subtotal										

Grand Total

Rating

10-49   Two reasons for a low score: (a) you don't like or get along with the people you work with OR (b) you haven't found your passion in life. If it's (a), ask yourself how can you change your relationships at the office. If it's (b), you can either look for ways to bring what you are passionate about into your career or you might need to change your career.

| 50-79 | You enjoy your work and have good relationships at the office. Focus on your lowest scores and put your heart into adding value in these areas as well. |
| 80-100 | You are singing on your way to work! |

In our quest to become women of value, most of us have three major roles to fulfill: wife, mother and career woman. In all these areas, becoming a woman of value is totally dependent upon our own actions, attitudes and behaviours. By making a conscious decision today that you will forever add value to the people and relationships in your life, you will inevitably become more valuable. You are able to do it. You want to do it. Do it!

 Rita Rocker is a national inspirational and educational speaker, Communications and Image Specialist with Transformation Academy, LLC and a Virtual Presentations Coach with the international coaching company, presentation gym. She is the author of *The Small Business Guide to Marketing Yourself for Success,* and a contributing author of *The Unstoppable Woman's Guide to Emotional Well Being.* She has appeared on national television and radio talk shows on self-esteem and communication. Rita is a former Mrs. Nebraska and Mrs. America contestant. She is active in numerous professional organizations, on the Board of the Small Business Association of the Midlands and a member of Phi Theta Kappa international honor society.

Rita provides life and career-transforming crash courses to mature teens and adults. These highly effective tools empower individuals to become more accomplished communicators, gain greater confidence in business and social graces and build productive relationships. She's an Image and Presentations Coach, and she's an expert in Communications.

Contact information:
www.transformationacademy.com
rita@transformationacademy.com
(402) 968-3250
http://womenforhire.com/career_experts/rita_rocker,
http://www.presentationgym.net/training/coach_bio/21

Chapter 9

A New You! Go From
Self Conscious to Self Confident
by: Rita Rocker

Once upon a time, there was a very smart, talented woman (we will call her Esther) who had dreams of living a purpose-filled life, physically and financially strong, with a wonderful family and friends. Because she was told from a young age that she didn't live up to her parents' expectations, she became very **self-conscious.**

> **Self-conscious**: awkward, ill at ease, insecure uncomfortable, embarrassed, unsure of oneself, timid.

Esther's heart longed to achieve her divine purpose but she was too focused on herself, her fears, and how inadequate she felt compared to others. There were a myriad of reasons and situations to blame for her unhappiness. These excuses kept her stuck, unable to venture too far from her "familiar places" where she could risk failure or rejection. Of course, that made her more angry and disappointed with herself. "What we believe to be true determines how we act and react to life," a friend said. "Why do you believe you only deserve the life of a chicken pecking for crumbs when you were meant to soar with the eagles?"

As Esther grew into a mature woman, she didn't realize that she, herself, was actually the CEO of her own life and was able to make her own life-changing decisions. She didn't see that she deserved her own personal metamorphosis that could bring her to the fulfillment of her dreams and ambitions.

One day Esther heard a still, small voice from heaven say, "My daughter, YOU are endowed with the same seeds of greatness as everyone else you have admired. Yes, you CAN move onward and upward…no matter what has transpired up to this point!" She was deeply moved by those words and so began the journey of achieving greater self-respect and making healthier choices. Esther created a more attractive, well-groomed appearance that continued to boost her confidence.   She took classes for personal and professional growth, and learned to laugh at herself.   Friends noticed a victorious smile and demeanor as she faced the challenges of life. She began to see her value, her positive attributes, and how much she had to offer as she pursued her divine destiny.

"No more self-fulfilling prophecies of failure for you dear," that voice whispered. "You are not hindered by lack of education, age, your financial situation, or anything else that could be an excuse. STOP! Right now, I want you to pick up all of those shattered pieces from your life. When you have gathered them all up, get away to a quiet place and create a beautiful picture of what you really want your life to be. Make a beautiful mosaic from all those pieces. Don't question or make excuses, just visualize and create without analyzing or asking how it can come about."

Esther said she had wasted too many years and was too self-conscious to get anywhere in life. Just then, a beautiful butterfly flew into her window and dropped a message on the bed. She couldn't believe her eyes! The message said: "Esther, it's time for YOUR Metamorphosis! Read on, dear child." So she read:

"You'd never guess what happened to a little worm one day. Her heart was filled with sadness as she inched along her way. "Oh, woe is me," she sadly cried, "how drab my life has been. No matter how I've tried and tried, it seems I just can't win.

I'm tired of being in the mud, of crawling on the ground. If I could soar through blue skies and walk or run around, I'm sure then I'd be happy and I could laugh and smile. Then joy and peace would come my way and life would be worthwhile."

Then, came a message floating in on a gentle breeze. It seemed to say, "Be patient and put your heart at ease. Just trust me for your future and let your old self die. Inside that lowly worm I've put a lovely butterfly!" And, then, as faith took over and possessed her every thought, She kept the vision in her mind, of the miracle to be wrought. And, daily, never doubting, she drew nearer to her goal, No longer sad, discouraged, her God was in control.

With one last mighty struggle for freedom from the past, she burst the bonds asunder that long had held her fast. Then, with delight that knew no bounds, she soared up toward the sky-- enraptured, happy, joyous--A lovely butterfly! **That is your hope...and your promise!**

Esther couldn't believe her eyes! She was ready to give up, discouraged, believing she was too self-conscious to accomplish anything significant or fulfill her purpose. Yet after she read that story, she knew she couldn't turn back. She remembered the Weeble dolls she played with as a little girl, the ones with the rounded bottoms that always bounced back up when they were pushed down. The voice softly said, "Esther, just like those Weebles, you may fall over but you can't fall down! You can conquer your fears and be a powerful woman if you trust Me. Just another two inches of soil needs to be dug up before you strike oil. Dig up the soil, plant those seeds of faith, and water them every day. You will see how beautiful you really can become, your roots strong and deep, and your beauty beyond compare. Esther, take My hand. It's never too late to get back up again. You may have been knocked down but you're not out for good. Be a Weeble, beautiful girl!!!"

Dear reader, how many times do we treat ourselves as if we are not as good as others and determine our value according to someone's opinion? Or never compliment ourselves for a job well done (or for the *effort* if the outcome wasn't what we hoped for)? Or are never satisfied with our work? Or dwell on our failures rather than our accomplishments? Do you realize that by dwelling on your failures, hurts, financial position or (fill in the blank), that you will actually draw more of the same to you? It's a proven scientific fact! The law of attraction, or sowing and reaping, brings into your life what you have sown by what you think and do every day.

Remember your significance has no bearing on what television, the fashion industry, or other's opinions have to say. No human being has the right to determine your value, worth, future or any other part of your life by their careless and insensitive *opinion*. It is a mere *incorrect* judgment **but God's opinion is the only one that truly matters...and He knows that everything you need is already within you!**

A trusted mentor once told me, "It is easy to live down to the self-fulfilling prophecies that we or others have placed on us. If we were told we would turn out all wrong, we ask ourselves what is the use in trying anyway? But if we are encouraged in our ability to accomplish a task, how many times do we succeed? There is so much power in the tongue to lift up or tear down! A person's life can literally be ruined by someone's sharp tongue *if* the recipient doesn't realize his or her value and takes those words to heart. We all know individuals who lived their whole lives going through one failure after another. Why? Because their future as a "failure" was ingrained into them from childhood by a parent, teacher, or peers. **Did you ever stop to think that**

you don't have to go through life that way? Be encouraged by the following two examples out of hundreds we could read about:

Sally Jessy Raphael: Well-recognized former NBC broadcaster. Although she graduated from Columbia University, she was told, "You have the perfect voice for broadcasting, but you should get a job as a secretary. We're not using women." As an unstoppable woman, she hosted one of the most popular talk shows for two decades.

Mary Kay Ash: The cosmetics tycoon, was told by her attorney weeks before she opened her first store, "Liquidate the business right now and recoup whatever cash you can. If you don't, you'll end up penniless." In 2003, this unstoppable woman was honored with the award of "Greatest Female Entrepreneur of American History" by a panel of academicians and business historians. Oprah Winfrey ranked second.

> *"If you are not being treated with love and respect, check your price tag. Perhaps you have marked yourself down. It's YOU who tells people what you are worth by what you accept. Get off the clearance rack & get behind the glass where the valuables are kept! Learn to value yourself. If you don't, no one else will!"*

- Author unknown

Moving to Self-Confidence: (confident about who you are, poised, sure of yourself, secure, positive)

It is NEVER too late to reinvent yourself!
Did you know that the most important thing a woman can wear is confidence? Well, let's get back to Esther's transformation and see how it applies to **your** life!

Esther began paying attention to the self-fulfilling prophecies she was living by and changed her inner dialogue after realizing she really was worthy of a good life. When phrases like, "you're not as good as your sister" or "you will never amount to anything" become ingrained in us,  they must be rooted up and replaced with the truth of our immeasurable value! Otherwise, we spend our whole life in either defeat---or strive to be a perfectionist, and that mindset becomes an endless battle of disappointment.

The next step Esther took toward gaining self-confidence was by associating with people who were loving, supportive, and positive. Anyone holding her back was no longer a part of her life! Esther began avoiding the trap of comparing herself to others. She no longer determined her value by her job, bank account, and lack of a college degree.

The same mindset applies to everyone reading this story. Realize that you each have your own unique abilities and purpose in life and don't cut yourself short by comparing your credentials to others instead of nourishing your own abilities. For example, someone's journalism degree may scare you from applying for a public relations job, but you excel in people skills that may far surpass hers. So you step out and go for it! Develop your abilities and use your energy to make them grow. Being concerned about what others accomplish doesn't get you anywhere, especially when it comes to achieving your divine purpose.

Yes, it can take a lot of effort, dedication and perseverance, however, you must continue on through any discouragement. Know that if you "expect" to fail, you will. "He who aims at nothing shall surely hit it every time." But if you plan to win, you will...when you head towards your focus. Esther began to practice this advice and found that even when she encountered obstacles (a disappointing job, failed relationship, financial roadblock), she became stronger and more powerful each time she faced a difficulty and bounced back into action. Even with her transformed mindset and new behaviors, her transformation was not complete until after her next dream finished showing her the way.

Esther's Dream: One night in a dream, Esther encountered a very loving, yet strong angel who said, "Just like you, everyone has many untapped resources. They possess talents and gifts both outwardly and inwardly. Talents like compassion, determination, good homemaking or organizational skills, being a hard worker, kindness to others, and an endless list of thousands of attributes."

Esther then looked down and noticed a caterpillar struggling to get free from its cocoon. As she fixed her gaze on that little creature's plight, to her amazement she saw the most beautiful butterfly emerge. Esther pondered over what she just witnessed. Like the painful struggles the caterpillar had gone through to reach its goal and become beautiful, Esther realized that all of the struggles she faced had been worth it too. Each struggle was instrumental in providing a valuable, life-changing lesson. Like the butterfly, she understood how her own metamorphosis was bringing freedom to soar high and lead others along this new path. Her new-found life and greater sense of confidence finally manifested because she never gave up!

The second part of Esther's dream took her to the sea, where she viewed a magnificent pearl laying at her feet. She had read that the only way a pearl comes into being is a result of the injury done to the oyster by the constant irritation of a sharp piece of sand. It is that gnawing pain inside the oyster that eventually produces the efforts to protect it, the result eventually being a pearl of great beauty and value. The angel then said, "Esther, you and every one of God's daughters are just like that pearl. You are able to make something beautiful out of your pain and fear. Now use this knowledge to guide other women down the same path. As you do, your confidence will soar even higher as you help change lives and fulfill your purpose! When Esther awakened from her dream, she felt a renewed sense of self worth, and she began the process of self healing.

> Note: Getting the pearl requires the oyster to be opened but despite the hardness of the oyster shell, they can be opened with ease. Oyster shells are held closed by a single muscle called the adductor. Oysters are opened using a thin knife to cut the adductor muscle. Once the adductor is cut, the shell falls open. Sometimes our "opening process" is difficult but the end result is beyond belief!

The Road to Self-Confidence is a slow, yet steady, progression.

First, you have to take your foot off the brake! Realize that you will sit in that same spot the rest of your life if you don't get back behind the wheel of your life. Proclaim, "I will not stop my journey too soon. It's time to get out and overcome every obstacle in my way!"

Here are some of the steps that you, can take:
o **Imagine yourself at your absolute best...the ideal you.**
   Act the part of the successful person you have decided to be. How are you dressed and what are you doing? Who would you like included in this picture? Envision yourself doing what you

need to do to reach your goal. Are you attending a class, working out and getting stronger, or taking a public speaking class? See yourself smiling, strong, and enjoying your outcome. See this happening every day and watch how fast life can change. Be mindful not to go back to all of the old patterns that didn't work.

- **It's NEVER too late to start over no matter what has happened to you. Your new life starts today!**
Remember the old saying, "If you always do what you've always done, you'll always get what you've always had." What holds you back? Do you need to start saying "no" if you are over committed trying to make everyone else happy? You know what you need! So rehearse your new role in life, starting now.

- **Move on now...not tomorrow!**
Look at each mistake only as a life lesson that shows you what to do differently next time. That includes forgiving yourself for your mistakes. Today is your new beginning – not when you lose weight and get into shape, or finally can afford the newer car or house, or get married, or have a better job.

- **Accept yourself as a beautiful creation who deserves self-respect...Always!**
On those days when you may not like yourself, look beyond your mirror and remember that you are made in God's image. That is the most powerful and beautiful image there is! Ask God to show you how you look *through* His eyes. Every morning offers us a chance to begin again...and again, and again. Build yourself up by speaking *respectfully* to, and about, yourself.

o **Examine your relationships.**
Destructive relationships destroy self-esteem. Constant negative feedback wears you down. Change can be frightening but very rewarding. Work on new friendships. It can change your life!

o **Become aware of what tapes are playing in your mind.**
Listen to your self-talk. We are what we think we are, whether that means a success, a failure, or a dynamic woman who can move mountains. Stop and listen to your internal tapes and keep ejecting the negative ones. When the music you are listening to begins to bother you, you change the CD. The same goes for your mind. Pop those positive CD's back in every time a negative thought creeps into your mind. It may take a lot of effort at first, however, watch your smile increase, your posture become more erect and see your relationships become even better!

o **Learn from your mistakes.**
I have had much pain and trauma in my life, and finally realized that those terrible mistakes gave me valuable lessons in wisdom. They have kept me sensitive and compassionate and steered me in a healthier, more productive direction. Keep growing into your beautiful, confident self. All that you need is already within you!

o **Be aware of the signals you are sending out!**
Remember that your appearance reveals so much about your self-Image and self-confidence. When conducting business, including professional social events, ensure that your appearance, wardrobe and grooming are exhibiting the kind of impression that you want to give to others. You appear more responsible and organized if you are all "pulled together." If associates see that you take pride in your appearance, they are

more likely to assume that you take pride in "*your*" work and "*their*" business as well. As you continue to enhance your professional presence, your confidence will continue to grow!

Get your foot off of that brake!! Hit the gas beautiful lady, hit the gas!!!

Let's sing, dance, and ride the roller coaster of life in high gear. We can choose to live life to the fullest! Be an Esther, Start NOW, from where you are, and make a brand new ending to the story of your life!

Ethel Maharg is the former mayor of the Village of Cuba, New Mexico, where she served in office for 10 years, three terms as mayor. She was the first elected woman mayor of Cuba. She has been privileged to address many audiences, such as the Sandoval County tourism conference, and has shared the same platform as Governors Gary Johnson, Bill Richardson, Senator Tom Udall, and in Washington Senators Pete Domenici and Jeff Bingaman.

Ethel's greatest passion is to help you discover yours. She loves to speak to audiences that desire to improve their station in life. She provides inspirational leadership training to help people in the achievement of their personal and professional goals.

Her mission is to empower individuals to find their purpose, and equip them to pursue it. To make a difference in every life she touches. She challenges everyone to live a life that is uncommon.

Ethel is an alumnus of University of Phoenix where she received her degree in business administration. She has owned and operated several small businesses, been an educator, worked with unions, and managed two branches for Wells Fargo.

Ethel is a proud member of the National Speakers Association, the Hispano Chamber of Commerce, and currently serves on a Women's Leadership Team for Women's Leadership Development at New Beginnings Church of God where she is an active member. She is a keynote speaker as well as a trainer. Her audiences love her openness and her no nonsense humorous approach. Ethel resides in Albuquerque, New Mexico with her husband of almost 28 years.

Contact information:
mayormaharg@hotmail.com

Chapter 10

Kick Fear's Butt!
by: Ethel R. Maharg

Leonardo DiCaprio said in an interview, "I like to do things that scare me," after a skydiving incident where his parachute didn't open and his instructor had to pull his emergency cord. After several adventures he said, "it makes you feel excited all over again to be alive." That's what I'm talking about!

We are going to kick fear's butt by first identifying what it is, where it comes from, how it works, and then outline a plan to overcome it.

Fear, as defined by Webster's Dictionary, is (1) an unpleasant often strong emotion caused by anticipation or awareness of danger (2) a state marked by this emotion. Fear in the most general term implies anxiety and usually loss of courage.

What is courage? Again, according to Webster, it's mental or moral strength to venture, persevere, and withstand danger, fear, or difficulty. So according to these definitions, the reason we have

fear, is because our mental state is not developed enough to prevent fear from gripping us, therefore paralyzing us.

In order to kick fear's butt you first need to understand what it is. Fear is insidious; it starts possibly with a suggestion of something going wrong or of some impending danger. It's like a cancer that has metastasized. It then grows into something that paralyzes us. It's like being bitten by a deadly poisonous snake that paralyzes the nervous system. First you feel the initial sting, and then little by little your body cannot move, your breathing slows down and eventually you die. While you may not die a physical death from fear, the effects of it can cause you to stop dead in your tracks. Fear can cause you to settle for less than you were created to be, therefore forfeiting your dreams.

Now let's talk about another aspect of fear that you might not have thought of. We have all heard of the acronym of F.E.A.R. meaning **F**alse **E**vidence **A**ppearing **R**eal. It is interesting to note that the word evidence is used because faith is rarely present in the presence of fear. The definition of faith is: "The substance of things hoped for; the evidence of things not seen." What is evidence? Well in a court of law evidence is proof. Evidence is an outward sign of what you believe to be true.

Fear and faith go hand in hand. Yes you read it right. As you look at the definitions of both fear and faith it can be summed up like this. Fear is faith moving in the wrong direction. Both fear and faith believe that something is going to happen and they move you in the direction of your most dominant thought. This being the case you need to decide (the operative word here being decide) what outcome you wish to have. You have to develop your thinking to a level where what you have most of, is faith.

Let's look at an example of what fear can produce in the story of Job in the Bible. He said something early on in the story "The thing that I feared most has come upon me." Job sacrificed daily for his children just in case they had sinned and God would be angry. He lived in fear. How do we know this? It is the first thing that came out of his mouth after all the calamities were reported to him.

This brings us to another point. You may be good at hiding your fears, but when push comes to shove, what is in your heart **will** come out of your mouth. It's just like an orange; when you squeeze it you will get orange juice. When you are squeezed, what is coming out of you and your mouth? This will give you an indication of what you fear.

Fear is a normal emotion. It warns us of impending danger, and sometimes it is warranted. It can keep us from potentially harmful situations. When we experience fear we need to stop and assess the situation to see if the fear we are experiencing is warranted. 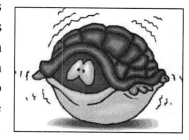 Is there really something that could harm you or are you allowing your emotions to run amok? You set on a course to do something then begin the roadblocks which generate fear. An example of this took place as I decided to write this chapter: I knew that this is what I am meant to do, but all of a sudden I began to think, "I don't know the first thing about writing a book, getting it published, and where am I going to get the money." I began to tell myself, "I'm not smart enough, talented enough, and rich enough and the list goes on." This is where fear began to take its nasty hold on me. My palms got sweaty, my breathing got shallow, and I ended up with a headache. I began an internal dialogue that was defeating and self sabotaging. But then I remembered that I am *indeed* an unstoppable woman with a story to tell, and my story is worth writing about. I had to kick fear right in the pants so this chapter could manifest.

As the definition of fear states, it is the *anticipation* of danger. Notice it didn't say that there *is* danger. At this point you need to look fear square in the face and say, "Who do you think you are trying to scare me?! Don't you know who you are talking to? I am wonderfully made, I can do all things, and whatever resources I need from the foundations of the earth before I was a twinkle in my Daddy's eye, God has already made preparations for me. Everything I need has already been supplied for me to fulfill my destiny." You may say this is a foolish thing to start saying, but I am telling you that if you don't you will be doomed to a life that is limited to your fears. Remember fear is not your friend. Burst out of fear and demand of life what is yours, because when you arrived on this earth you came fully equipped to do that which you were created for. You are the actress in an Oscar nominated movie. How do you want it to play out? Write how you want your life to turn out, and rehearse the script of your life every day. You were created for greatness so live like you are!

The gospel group Point of Grace has a song called Fearless Heart, and it states, "I want to live with a fearless heart. Courage that's coming from trust in God. It's constantly guiding me though the road may seem dark." The bible says that fear is not from God, in fact it says in 1Timothy 1:7 – "I have not given you a spirit of  fear, but of power, of love and of a calm sound mind." Hmmm, if God didn't give it to us where did it come from? It comes from several places. Some of it is learned, some is instilled by others, and it can come from unpleasant experiences where we failed. We are afraid of the unknown, and of circumstances that are beyond our control that seem insurmountable, and we feel overwhelmed by it all. It comes because you believe you have to do things on your own and there is no one to help, when this is not the truth. You are never alone and all you have to do is reach out and God is going to be there.

Fear comes from other people. Often well intentioned people will hinder you by telling you to play it safe and don't take any chances. In essence what they are doing is instilling fear, therefore stealing your dreams. Other not so well intentioned people will say "who do you think you are, attempting to do that difficult task?" That person may even be you. Nelson Mandela says *"Our deepest fear is not that we are inadequate. Our deepest fear is that we are powerful beyond measure. We ask ourselves, Who am I to be brilliant, gorgeous, talented, fabulous? Actually, who are you not to be? We were born to make manifest the glory of God that is within us. And as we let our own light shine, we unconsciously give other people permission to do the same."* Who are you, and who do you think you are? I will tell you who you are. You are a masterpiece in the making, you are beautiful beyond compare and gifted with the ability to do the impossible.

So how do we move from fear to faith? I've outlined for you seven steps to kick fear's butt, and overcome fear.

1. **Determine what you want, not what you may be afraid of.**

   For example, if you are looking at a stack of bills, you will need to set them aside mentally. This does not mean to be irresponsible or hiding your head in the sand. Realize that if you are continually staring at the problem, it is difficult to focus on a solution. So set the bills aside for a while to give yourself time to formulate a workable plan. The same goes for health issues. Acknowledge that you have been given a report. You do not have to make it your own. I cringe when I hear people say "_my_ diabetes or _my_ cancer," so on and so forth. When you take ownership of something, all your thoughts and energy will go towards nourishing it, causing it to grow just like any baby that you feed. Whenever you feed and nurture a baby it will grow, and so will your problem if you feed and nourish it.

There is a story of a man who long ago raised dogs to fight. Every week when he would choose the dog he thought would win and it did. This went on for some time until someone asked him, "How do you do that? How do you always pick the winning dog?" Without hesitation he said, "Oh that's easy. I pick the one I've been feeding." Whatever you focus on is going to win every time.

2. **Know Your 'Why.'**
We have all heard of stories about mothers who miraculously lifted cars off of their babies to save their life. Did she have super strength? No, she had a 'why' that was bigger than her fear. She didn't have time to allow fear to stop her from achieving her objective. She had a mission, and too much time spent thinking could mean the life of her child will end. Often times fear creeps in when we think too much instead of acting on what we know to do. If your reason for doing what you do isn't big enough, any little problem can to stop you. Develop something that is bigger than you with a reason so compelling that nothing will stop you. It needs to involve the possibility of impacting several if not thousands of lives if you dare to live your dream.

3. **Develop a plan**. The reason that fear often creeps in is that there is no clear cut plan for where you want to go. The first thing is to get a plan with some clearly defined goals, a time to reach them, and steps to get there. There are many goal setting programs; choose one that is best for you and your 'why.'

4. **Seek council**. Seek out someone who has been where you are and has gone where you want to be. You could learn from your own mistakes, but why would you want to when

you can shorten the process by learning from the mistakes and pain of others? Although the saying, "Experience is the best teacher," applies in most cases, it just makes better sense to learn something from someone who can help you avoid unnecessary hardships. I always say that I like to surround myself with people who are a whole lot smarter than me.

5. **Lighten up.** Life pretty much guarantees tough challenges before it's all over, so have a little fun along the way. Take time to smell the roses, if you will. Sometimes people say one day we're going to look back at this and laugh about it. If at some point you are going to laugh why don't you just go ahead and do it now? We get so caught up in making a living that we forget to live. My daughter had to remind me one day when she said, "On your deathbed are you going to say I'm sure glad I paid that bill on time or are you going to be able to look back at all the good times you had with your friends and family?" Pretty smart for a 26 year old! When you are afraid, it keeps you from having fun because you spend all your time being fearful that you are too young, too old, not as beautiful, talented, or have enough money. None of these reasons are enough to keep you from enjoying your life. It is short so enjoy it!

6. **Take time for your dreams**. In order to kick fear's butt you are going to need to make time for dreaming. Get a vision of the life you want and play it on the screen of your mind daily. In the book 'Think and Grow Rich', Napoleon Hill recommends that you spend time visualizing your dream in the morning and the evening. If you don't currently have success, spend time in the world that you want. What does this have to do with fear? Everything; because fear is about something in your future. When you

can paint a vivid picture and focus on it for long lengths of time two things will happen. You will begin to move in the direction of your dream and move away from the fear.

7. **Get rid of your excuses and just do it!** There is nothing

like taking action that will energize you and give you the strength to get out of the pit of fear. The worst thing that can happen to you is you fall flat on your face…and then you get up and try it again.   I have a friend that has always wanted to work in the financial services industry, yet after several years she has yet to take her insurance exam. One day I asked her why and she didn't have an answer. Then I shared with her why I believed she had not done so. It's because it was her way out and people would excuse her, making it ok for her not being where she says she wants to be. Her fear of success in this instance has caused her to make excuses in order to keep her in a 'safe' place mentally. However, financially she is nowhere near where she would like to be.

Most people believe that the worst thing that can happen is you fall flat on your face. Actually, the worst thing that can happen is that you never become what you were intended to become, and you never fulfill your destiny, and the world is not better because you didn't try.

When it comes to relationships, again you must focus on the best parts of a person like their kindness, timeliness, order, being a good provider, etc. If things have gone south and your fear is that it is over, know this: nothing is too late unless you two choose not to make things work.

This goes for anything, not just relationships. There may have been horrendous crimes committed against you as a child, and if this is the case you have more to overcome. But I have seen great people like Beth Moore, Joyce Meyer, and Paula White who suffered sexual abuse as little girls, make great strides in their lives. They had to make some difficult choices, but now their success speaks for itself. James Robison is a product of rape. He said on his television program that he still suffers from feelings of unworthiness, yet he presses on. The key here is to keep moving past the pain. Don't park there, worse yet don't dwell there or make it your home mentally. Dwelling on something is thinking of something over and over, you in essence live there. Where are your thoughts living?

My biggest fear is not that I will fail but that I will not fulfill my purpose. Therefore, I have to do everything possible to see to it that I do not die with my story still in me.

Let me encourage you with this: the world needs the gifts that you have and if you allow fear to rule your life then the world will be poorer for it. But if you dare to kick fear's butt, the world will be richer because you made the choice to be all you were created to be.

Connie Brubaker began her training and speaking business because she is passionate about the power of relationships to make a business successful. Connie is the owner of Integrity Training Solutions since 1999 where she helps businesses get and keep customers through leadership, customer service, marketing to women, and sales training. She has worked with clients such as Austin Radiological Association, Newpark Drilling, Infiniti, and Sharp Propane. Connie discovered training tools that embraced the philosophy that contributed to her 20 years of success owning and operating a multi-million dollar company, which consisted of three Kentucky Fried Chicken franchises.

As part of her strategy to dominate the industry, Connie was the creator of the KFC chicken strips, which generated one billion dollars in first year sales internationally. Not only did she double sales in all three restaurants, she forced the closing of virtually all her competition.

In her keynotes and training, Connie is able to use her real world experiences to convey her messages in her keynotes about customer service, leadership, developing sales ability, attracting and keeping the female client. She also inspires women on being a resilient woman. Connie is known for her humor, sincerity, knowledge, and ability to connect with people.

Contact information:
Connie@ConnieBrubaker.com
512-346-7270
www.ConnieBrubaker.com

Chapter 11
What Men Really Want
by: Connie Brubaker

Unstoppable women have learned to be resilient, overcome, pursue, persist, love ourselves, believe, achieve, manage, maintain, nurture, accept, assert, communicate, and so much more. As women, we are learning to understand ourselves. Part of the road is to understand others, including men. Half of the population is male and whether we are in a personal or business relationship, we must understand how men think and feel. Women place their relationships with others as a high priority; the ease with which we work, play, manage, parent, love, motivate, and accept others will move us forward more quickly.

It is not always politically correct to state that men and women are different and we do share a lot of the same needs, but the way men and women go about attaining their needs can be quite different. Women, for hundreds of years, have fought hard for equality. I personally have contributed to this battle in the workplace and at home. I remember teaching my son that cooking, washing dishes, and doing laundry are not women's work. Also, my daughter understands that there is equal opportunity to mow the yard and take out the trash. There is a common debate that asks the question, are children more influenced by their home environment in their upbringing (nurture) or are they more affected by the internal genetic code (nature)? Ask most mothers about their infant son or daughter and you will hear that baby boys and girls behave very differently from birth. Is it because we act differently to a baby wrapped in a pink blanket versus a blue blanket? Scientific research reveals that as early as three days old, a baby girl holds eye contact twice as long as an infant boy with many other tests supporting the natural tendencies.

Science supports observations of the human anatomy that is made up of chromosomes, hormones, and brain structure that create our gender code. The chromosomes determine whether the fetus is male or female. After about six weeks after conception, the Y chromosome begins producing a prenatal testosterone that contributes to the traits of: aggressiveness, self-assertiveness, the drive for dominance, competitiveness, risk-taking, and thrill-seeking as studied by Dr. Moire & David Jessel in ***Brain Sex: The Real Difference Between Men and Women.*** Some women have higher levels of testosterone and may be more independent and self-assured. Higher levels of testosterone show that men and women score higher on spatial, mechanical, and math ability. As women reach middle age, the increase of assertiveness could be attributed to a boost in testosterone. And I thought that women in menopause simply do not care as much what others think of them.

As women, we are very acquainted with the female hormone, estrogen that produces the feelings of nesting and nurturing. The hormone called progesterone creates the parenting instinct. Another hormone that is dominant in women is serotonin, which creates feelings of calm and wellbeing. Most unstoppable women I know could use an extra dose of serotonin!

Neuroscientists have studied the brain and can view the way the brain functions. They have determined that there are differences between the sexes in the brain tissues, fibers, and activity in the hemispheres. Women use both the left and right side of the brain together while men primarily show use of the right hemisphere. Science reflects so many ways the physiological differences contribute to the way the genders have different preferences, abilities, and priorities. Biology helps to explains some of the reasons that men frustrate women.

Aside from science, most women recognize that we are different from men, but the question is how to respond to these differences that will help to get us what WE want. Women talk about men being: jerks, creeps, brutes, wimps, clueless, and pains; but we must deal with men almost every day of our lives. The goal is to learn about what men want so we can co-exist together. It is time to take the power that you have within you to improve your relationships with men.

WHAT MEN REALLY WANT:

RESPECT: Men would rather feel unloved than inadequate and disrespected. Men have been told from childhood not to cry, to be strong and to be self-reliant. Many men find their identity and self-worth in their work and the ability to protect and provide for their family. Men feel a strong drive to produce and provide. Women often fail to appreciate this drive in their husband, both privately and publicly. Shaunti Feldhahn's research indicates that men would rather sense the loss of love from their wives than to be disrespected by them. A man often shows anger or avoidance when criticized by his wife, though he may not use these words. Men have a lot of pressure to perform at work and at home. They often feel quite vulnerable in their role as a husband or father. They need support when they are feeling failure. As women we should show our belief in their ability to succeed.

Honorable men are protectors and would love to be our knight in shining armor and place us on pedestals. Women have become so self-reliant and feel that we can handle responsibility by ourselves, without asking for help, because we are capable. We often feel overwhelmed and overstressed because we have so many chores on our to-do list. Our men would appreciate the opportunity to "man up" by asking for their help. We as unstoppable women need to allow men to help us so that we can find success in what we want to achieve. Women can help men feel valued, respected, and honored by showing kindness and love. They need to hear appreciation loud and often for the difficult roles they play as providers or leaders.

TRUE STORY: A first-time father was so excited about taking his newborn baby home from the hospital. He held his precious girl while cooing and snuggling with her. As he was placing his daughter for the first time ever in the car seat, he was corrected on the way baby was slouching. His masculine response was so quick and obvious as he backed away from the scene and became an observer instead of a participant. This young man already felt inadequate and unsure so an encouraging and supportive remark on what he did properly would have given him confidence in his role as an involved and eager father.

How do you show significant men in your life that you respect them for their roles? What could you do or say to reinforce positive performance?

_____

_____

_____

_____

AFFIRMATION: Men want to be admired both privately and publicly. When they are recognized for their efforts, men thrive and strive to be better, stronger, kinder, wiser, caring, and helpful. A man is attracted to a woman that admires him and shows her approval of his attributes. Men need appreciation, encouragement, and acceptance to do things their way and when those acknowledgements are generously given, many men will do even more. Research has shown that behavior we want repeated should be recognized and rewarded, whether it is in the classroom, office, or at home. When women focus and point out the positives attributes of men, a deeper connection and appreciation results.

TRUE STORY: Jim is a marathon runner, weight lifter, and exercise fanatic. He takes pride in being in excellent shape and spends hours each week running and comes home drenched in sweat. He lifts weights and exercises in the garage. His wife, Mary, stood in the garage and watched him while complimenting him on the difficulty and number of his push-ups and his amazing "pecs." Not only did he appreciate her admiration for his dedication, but the very next day he came into the living room in his work-out clothes and asked Mary if she wanted to watch him do his push-ups.

Women miss so many opportunities to appreciate men – we are more likely to say "yuck, you are sweaty, don't touch me" or "I could use some help around here and you are spending hours on your dumb exercises."

What ways does the important man in your life excel?

_____

_____

_____

_____

What have you said or done to show that you appreciate this behavior?

_____

_____

_____

_____

QUIET TIME: Many men like to zone out at the end of a workday by silently heading to the couch with the remote or reading the newspaper, taking a nap, or playing a computer game. Men like to deal with stress by avoidance or distraction. Women like to de-stress from the day by talking and sharing. Many women want to hear about their husband's day and talk about their own. Women use up to 20,000 words each day. A man utters between 2000 – 4000 words in a day; 1000 -2000 vocal sounds, and makes a mere 2000 – 3000 body language signals. His daily average adds up to around 7000 communication words – around 1/3 of the output of a woman. This difference becomes pronounced at the end of the day when a man and a woman arrive home after a long day of work. He has completely used his "words" for the day and has no desire to communicate anymore. While some women may have used their quotient of words and is okay with the quiet, a stay-at-home mom may have used only 3000 words and has 17,000 left to use.

Men need the quiet to solve problems. Men can sit together in a meeting and problem-solve with total silence and be very comfortable. In fact, if you observe many of their favorite quiet past-times, such as fishing, hunting, golfing or watching a sports game, they have very little communication going on.

A woman should observe a man's desire to read the paper without seeing it as rejection. And a man can understand a woman's desire to talk without feeling it is an intrusion. We have differences and when we recognize and accept that fact, we don't have to take things personally and instead find a compromise.

TRUE STORY: Beth is frustrated that her teenage son, Drew, does not share his life with her except for single word responses to her questions about school, friends, or sports. She sits across the table from this uncommunicative male with hardly a word exchanged as he greedily eats his meal. Beth is disappointed in the relationship with her son because her daughter expounds on every part of her life. When Beth starts driving Drew to the orthodontist, she realizes on this 45-minute trip, he begins to slowly open up. She observes that when they are sitting side-by-side focused on another activity, such as driving, that he feels more open and willing to share. Beth realizes that she and Drew bond when they play electronic games or watch sports together.

How do the men in your life communicate?

_____

_____

_____

_____

How could you help communication improve?

_____

_____

_____

_____

PRIDE: Men reflect pride in many ways – they want the corner office, the fastest and shiniest car, the latest technology, and an attractive wife. Men are always conscious of where they stand compared to other men. Their goal is to be admired or regarded as superior. With men, when they say "get ahead"; they actually mean to get ahead of others. Men are always looking in comparative terms: higher/lower; faster/slower, or bigger/smaller. Men think competition is a good thing because it is fun and strengthens weaknesses. Even men's friendships can be competitive as they jest with put-downs and boasting. I always chuckle at men's advertising that shows the boyish ways of men.

Many men also take pride in their wife's appearance. We have all heard the term trophy wife. If you ever look at the wives or girlfriends of professional athletes, they are gorgeous with amazing bodies. These women: are status symbols, just like a Ferrari or a Rolex watch. These perfect 10's are attracted to these stars because of their power and money.

Men are very visual and everyday they see attractive women in the office, stores, and soccer fields. The top magazine subscriptions for men are Playboy and Penthouse; while for women it is Better Homes & Garden. Many wives can become so involved in being a mother, as well as: chauffer, cook, maid, and nurse that she loses herself. Some women quit making an effort during the childrearing years and then wonder after the children leave home why she and husband have grown so far apart. Most men do not expect their women to look perfect but instead to be his girlfriend and make him proud when he introduces her to others because of her confidence and style.

TRUE STORY: Lisa was asked for a divorce from her husband because he had fallen out of love with her. During each of her three pregnancies, she had gained more and more weight. Lisa had not taken time to take care of herself and rarely got out of her sweat suit, or wore make-up. After the divorce, Lisa immediately makes her own needs a priority as she loses weight, shops for new clothes and takes time for hair and make-up. She looks in the mirror and likes her image and the control she has taken of her life. She gains new confidence and re-captures the essence of who she is. Lisa begins going out with friends for happy hour and meeting new men. Lisa knows that she did too little, too late in her marriage and now she is taking the effort to be sexy and flirtatious with a total stranger, instead of the man she promised to love and honor.

Do you invest in yourself? What could you do to improve your appearance, self-esteem or the dynamics of your relationship?

_____

_____

_____

_____

DIRECT COMMUNICATION: A man values "report talk" so much more than "relationship talk." A man appreciates conversations that stay on the subject. Have you ever noticed that a man's sentences are much shorter and have a clear point and conclusion? Men have difficulty following women's convoluted conversation and may lose interest and not hear what she is saying. The majority of women identify the biggest failing of their husbands and boyfriends as the reluctance to talk. Women can talk about 3 subjects at a time that are connected to her while a man is confused and befuddled. In the humorous book *Why Men Don't Listen and Women Can't Read Maps* by Barbara & Allan Pease, they state that "women can speak and listen simultaneously, while at the same time accusing men of being able to do neither."

Men appreciate when women are direct and to the point. Women so often use hints at what she wants and become frustrated by the lack of response. Ask for what you want directly and factually with the exact action required. For example, if a woman wants to have more romance in the relationship, she might request flowers, a card, or a love note. The saying around my house is "ask for what you want, you just might get it."

TRUE STORY: A woman desired health insurance from her employer. She kept mentioning the health issues of her child and the frequent and expensive physician visits. The boss heard that she needed more time away from the office and a raise. He ignored her hints. For years, both were frustrated with the working relationship and neither felt appreciated. When she directly asked him about benefits, he agreed that she was a valuable employee and that they would enroll her in the insurance program.

Do you feel that you are being listened to and heard by men? How could you talk differently so that your message is heard more directly?

_____
_____
_____
_____

Is there a request that you have been hinting about that you could state more intentionally? Write it down in a way that a man might respond in a positive way.

_____
_____
_____
_____

SEX: Men bond through being physically connected. The act of making love is how a man feels that you love him and saying no often makes a man feel that he is undesirable and unloved. A woman wants to know that she is the only one he loves by romancing her. A woman can be resentful of an inconsiderate remark or action days before a man initiates sex and he doesn't even realize that she is turned off and is holding on to her power. Smart women know that if she delivers in the bedroom, more often than not, she will get what she wants from her man. If she is amorous and adventurous in the bedroom, the more he may cherish her. The end result will be increased intimacy.

TRUE STORY: A realtor shared the story of showing a house to a couple. The husband, Bob, was taking issue with the layout of the house and the paint colors. The wife was becoming aggravated because this was the house of her dreams. She leaned into Bob seductively and whispered in his ear. Bob turned to the realtor and said "let's make an offer."

When was the last time that you made the first move in or out of the bedroom? What could you do to spice up your love life? List your ideas here and get started today.

_____

_____

_____

_____

CONCLUSION: When women and men understand the origin of our differences, we will find it easier to live with them. Men want respect, achievement and sex whereas women treasure relationships, stability and love. Though women feel that we have come a long way, baby, we are still struggling to understand each other. Be the first one to affirm, listen and accept, even when it seems not to work. Try for 30 days and see the difference in the dynamics of your relationships.

"If you treat him like a king, he will treat you like a queen." (Menorat HaMaor)

I wish you fulfilling connections where both men and women feel valued, complete, and respected. As an unstoppable woman, we are smart, intuitive, and powerful. We can have all the things that our heart desires and deserves.

Da-Nay "The Conquering Coach" Macklin is an Entrepreneur, Author, Speaker, Certified Life Coach and Career Consultant. She specializes in life purpose and transitional coaching providing her clients the luxury of being able to live life by design rather than default.

Da-Nay has a Bachelors Degree (BS) in Business Management from the University of Illinois at Chicago. She received her coach training and Certified Christian Life Coach (CCLC) certification from the Professional Christian Coaching and Counseling Academy (PCCCA). She is a member of Coach Training Alliance (CTA).

Da-Nay is the Founder and President of Conquer All Odds Coaching, Inc., where she is dedicated and passionate in assisting clients to design individualized lifestyles based on their passion and purpose. With Coach Da-Nay you will be equipped and empowered to successfully navigate changes and transitions while breaking free of any obstacles potentially holding you back from the life you desire to live.

Da-Nay also holds many leadership positions to include: Vice President of the Speakers Authors and Publishers Association (SPAA), Board Member of Women of Vision & Destiny Ministries (WOVD), Career Facilitator at the Dunamis Woman Life Coaching Institute, and a member of the National Association of Professional Women (NAPW). She is also a contributor to numerous publications including: the Junior Achievement's "Ask the Expert" program, Dunamis Woman Magazine, Amateur Sports News Network's "Coaches Corner", and her proprietary monthly newsletter "Life Purpose Tips".

Contact information:
1-888-656-9970
wwww.conquerallodds.com

Chapter 12

Confront Your Past, Conquer Your Present
by: Da-Nay Macklin

You Cannot Conquer What You Will Not Confront!

"If only I could be smarter, more attractive, height-weight proportionate, wealthy...*then* maybe just then I would put an end to being so critical of myself". Sound familiar? You may be wishing your situation was different for whatever reason. Wouldn't it be nice to borrow Cinderella's fairy Godmother who could wave her magic wand or sprinkle a little pixie dust and *poof!* Be gone all of your stinking thinking! All negative self-talk would be a matter of the past and finally restored with the mentality of an Unstoppable Woman. How nice would that be? The Unstoppable Woman I speak of is one who will no longer allow herself to play victim while a victorious life awaits her; for she is more than a conqueror...for she is YOU!

In this chapter *we* (you are not alone in "this") will end emotional self-inflicted pain and stress through focusing on how to eliminate the detrimental pattern of not letting go of our past, and blaming ourselves for every misfortune. It is my goal for you to go from self-sabotaging to self-strengthening habits through exploring the importance of:

1. Not Letting Your Past Define You Nor Dictate Your Future. (Self-Reflection)
2. Not Being Puzzled by Your Past. (Self-Discovery)
3. Living Life by Design NOT Default. (Self-Transformation)

Before we explore the above outline, let me start by disclosing a few items to you. I am not exempt from the above and Lord knows I've had my share of pit falls and pity parties resulting from trials and tribulations of the past. Perhaps you too have said, "been there and done that", only to return back to that same low valley. I too have visited many valleys, and want you to know there is *value in the valley!* I wish to share the value I have found in my valleys along my journey. Throughout this chapter you may discover my transparency in sharing parts of my life with the purpose of your benefit intended. It is of the utmost importance that you become acquainted with me and my past journey. Before doing so, please know this chapter is one hundred percent all about <u>YOU</u> and not me!

How many times have you overheard or maybe even been part of a conversation amongst a group of women, where they're "sizing up" another woman simply by looking at her in the *present* completely oblivious to her *past*? One name comes to mind as a prime example of such conversations. Who you may ask? Oprah Winfrey. She did not start where she is today and the same holds true for me. During speaking engagements the presenter typically announces *part* of my biography that reads "Powerhouse Professional, Entrepreneur, Certified Life & Career Coach, Empowerment Speaker, and Published Writer." The announcer is simply reading present day accomplishments. Now ask that same announcer to read my life biography with a focus on my past. Wow how the story changes drastically, not to

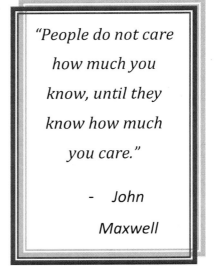

"People do not care how much you know, until they know how much you care."

- John Maxwell

mention the audience's facial expressions. Upon sharing my past they are in disbelief, as if it does not match the present day person staring them in the eye. I wish to invite you on a *brief* trip down memory lane into my painful and stressful past to prove a few points going forward in this chapter.

As we journey through this chapter, from the bottom of my heart please trust and know that I care about you and your emotional well-being! I know from experience how depressed, hopeless and discouraged a person can feel after a painful event or in my case a series of painful events.

I grew up on the south side of Chicago in poverty with a single mother until I moved out at 16 years of age. Initially my father denied I was his daughter, but thankfully he came around later in my life. Shortly before my 13th birthday, I seem to recall my mother's world crashing down resulting from the death of my grandmother. For many years my mother made a decent living as a Licensed Practical Nurse. Her occupation required annual renewals for her to remain actively working.

In an effort to comfort her during her loss she turned to alcohol just like most of the people in our neighborhood. She then made a *choice* to participate with the neighborhood alcoholics and spend countless hours drinking with them. It was a memorable time, because prior to this my mom was always a sweet woman to me but then as she would drink she became very abusive. It was like living with Dr. Jekyll and Mr. Hyde; I never knew who I was coming home to. Can you imagine that? I recall being mentally and physically assaulted by my mother whenever she would drink and that was quite often during this time as well as later on in life. She would say such things as, "you will never amount to anything" and that is on the milder side of some of her statements followed by kicking me out onto the street.

Her judgment became severely impaired due to her alcohol problem; allowing for a male stranger to easily befriend her with the intent of molesting me. Over the next few years, we were living off welfare and being evicted annually as the verbal and physical violence continued. It took a toll on me to the point of no return where I decided to end my life. I attempted three times to commit suicide but all three were failed attempts...obviously, and I thank God for canceling the devil's plans and now fulfilling His purpose upon my life!

Because of these episodes I grew up believing that what I endured was my fault, and I blamed myself throughout the years of these misfortunes. As a result of this I perceived myself to be a "bad person" and was not worthy of the good things in life. We will reference the negative effects of comparing one's life later in this chapter.

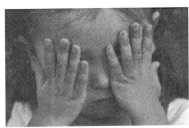

What was self-esteem and confidence? As I had no clue, considering mine were at an all time low, and my outlook on life was beyond depressing. I'm happy to say TODAY this is far from my view of life! Now the embarrassment continued following me right into adulthood sending me into the depths of despair to survive this stress, pain, and depression. I became resentful towards my mom for not protecting me from herself and others. Majority of my teen years and some of the twenties were consumed with sadness, guilt, hurt, and anger. The stronger I held on to the past, the unhappier I found myself. The past consumed me like a burning inferno!

Allowing your past experiences to have such power over your present existence is a sure way to destroy any hope of your present let alone future. You must comprehend what happened in the past is done and there is NOTHING you can do about it. Regardless how long you harp on it, it will never go away until YOU make a conscious decision for it to go away. Take a moment for yourself right now after reading the following question; temporarily for this time close the book and ponder, "who or what is in control of my life right now, today?" (Take as much time as you need.)

Ladies does it not seem as though we beat ourselves up for every little flaw no matter how big, medium, or small? At the end of the day, none of this chastisement is serving us in becoming victorious or being happy in our daily lives. I hear women say, who can blame us for being so hard on ourselves considering? I don't know about you, but I'm willing to guess if your plate is not already full it is overflowing. Perhaps you can relate to the following, which is a snapshot of my life for illustration intentions. I call it prioritizing the priorities! I try to make sure my mornings start with a spiritual peace (if not interrupted by my little princess), followed by getting her ready, fed, and dropped off to school. Now career enters the picture, calls and emails to reply to, projects and deadlines to attend to. Hopefully get some time in at the gym. Pick up the princess from school, make dinner, feed the family and the fur babies, shower the princess and get her ready for bed, pay bills, organize the social calendar, make time for the hubby and now back to work for me and hopefully a shower let alone a bubble bath☺. Now the fun part, get up and do it all again the next day!

It's the job or career, husband or boyfriend, child or children; health status, organizational commitments . . . our laundry list is never ending (some of it our own fault...yeah, I said it). Some of us are not only bringing home the bacon, but putting it in the pan and frying it too, but then we're expected to have mind blowing sex with our spouses while catering to their egos, get the house attended to including, but not limited to grocery shopping, laundry,

149

housework and have it all done in a day...ladies, Rome was not built in a day and neither were we! Then we have society bombarding us to look like some "perfect" airbrushed model on a magazine with a firm butt & boobs and flawless skin. Then we compare ourselves and once we do, we feel "less than," what "appears" to be the norm. The demands of present day life makes it seem as if we should be flattered to be pulled in several different directions all at the same time. After all don't we wear a big "S" on our chest, and respond to being "Superwoman"? Well, I say enough is enough with all these fairytales!

Once upon a time, there lived a little princess named Makayla who feared Monsters. Makayla is my beautiful daughter and of course my little princess who developed the F.E.A.R. (**F**alse **E**vidence **A**ppearing **R**eal) of "monsters". She was afraid to open her closet at night, in fear "monsters" would  approach. After speaking with her pediatrician we learned the following. In her head, a monster is a real something, that intends to harm her or loved ones. Kids create monsters because of their personal experiences that show them how people can behave in a painful manner toward one another. After explaining clearly the difference between pretend vs. reality, I stood by her side to confront those scary monsters hiding in her closet. I'm happy and proud to report that she has conquered those monsters...her fear! Maybe you and many other women are just like my daughter. Has someone or something in your past caused you pain?

Unfortunately or fortunately (depending on your perspective) we all experience various levels of pain. Perhaps someone you loved abandoned you? Maybe even your own children or stepchildren have disrespected you? Have your parents been emotionally and/or physically violent to you? Have you been a "victim" of domestic violence? The list of wrong doings can be never ending, but at the same time, painful memories need healing.

Such unpleasant experiences cause a great deal of pain that we feel inside and tend to struggle in letting it go in order to believe the life you DESERVE is possible. The greater the pain you bear only means a stronger desire to achieve an emotional sense of balance. So recognize the pain and stress you face as your brain's way of saying, "I desire to feel better." Even though right now you may feel weak and worn; you do have the power inside of you to make this transformation take place. We have an instinctive ability that we must learn to listen to in order to transform our lives and free ourselves. This transformation only takes place when you make the decision to be the **victor** and not the *victim*! The pain and stress of the past can no longer hurt you. Below are a few things I wish for you to contemplate:

- How much longer do I plan to stay idle in my emotional despair hoping for a better way?
- How much longer do I continue to feel jealous or spiteful of others who are "succeeding" and moving forward with their lives?
- How much longer do I want to feel mediocre every day that goes by?
- When dreadful things occur in the past do you buy into the belief that your past dictates your future and it's typical to be ruined for life?

Ladies please do trust, know, and embrace that *you are not what you feel, but rather what you believe.* TODAY you are going to consciously make a choice to become *victorious* in the present or remain a *victim* of your past. Life is change, growth is optional, the power to choose resides in you, but you must choose wisely! It is truly my belief and passion in life for you to realize that YOU are more than a conqueror whether you realize it or not! Conceivably this may appear to be surreal for you, but let me reassure you that by the end of this chapter and book you will understand this belief.

What exactly does it mean to conquer- what is your own personal definition? An online definition reads: To overcome or surmount by physical, mental, or moral force. In plain terms I agree with this definition. As for me, to be more than a conqueror you must first start with conquering yourself before conquering the world. *"It is better to conquer yourself than to win a thousand battles. Then the victory is yours. It cannot be taken from you, not by angels or by demons, heaven or hell"* – Buddha.

I absolutely love the above quote! Allow me to reiterate, You Cannot Conquer What You Will Not Confront. Would you agree with this statement? What do you need to confront in order to conquer? Conquering oneself is about establishing an inner victory. One key ingredient to living a victorious life is to live as an overcomer. We as women face so much adversity to overcome that our past is only one piece of the puzzle. Other puzzle pieces include, but are not limited to the following:

1. Discrimination (Racial, Sexual, Religious, Height/Weight, Social, and Occupational.
2. The proverbial "glass ceiling" for equal pay, positions, and promotions. Not to mention just securing meaningful work.
3. Powerful women being categorized as "bitchy"
4. The guilt associated with either working outside of the home or working in the home (some women know this as being on duty 24/7) in order to care for our children.
5. Harassments (Sexual, Psychological, Cyber, and Workplace).
6. Abuse (Physically and/or sexually).

7. Depression (types prevalent in women: Premenstrual Syndrome (PMS), Premenstrual Dysphoric Disorder (PMDD), Postpartum Depression, and Premenopausal Depression).

8. Securing retirement since we earn less, typically lag in savings and financial awareness but live longer than men.

9. Foreign Country Discrimination Sex trafficking (young as 5 years old), not "allowed" to speak to men (unless related), vote, drive, publically reveal their face, denied education, husbands can deny their wives food, shelter, and abuse her and she can't leave, and these are just to name a few.

Around the age of ten I can recall my mother putting together puzzles. As a child she would invite me to sit alongside of her and participate. Although it was quite testing at times, it was an obstacle to conquer! I would celebrate the little success in rejoicing at finding a piece that fit, as it turned out to be quite rewarding.

While reflecting on this childhood experience it showed several similarities between puzzles and life. Every puzzle piece plays such a critical part in the big picture. In our lives, it is people and events that play the critical parts. As with pieces in a puzzle, each one of us is so unique and special in our own way.  On the surface we may appear alike. However, there are no two just alike; even our fingerprints are individually constructed. Maybe it's our differences that make us fit.

Have you ever done a puzzle? If so, then you know what it is like to spend so much time looking for one very specific puzzle piece. In my mind as a little girl I really thought I knew what it looked

153

like, but as you know looks can be deceiving. Even though it appeared to be so obvious…I just could not find it! How could I allow myself to become so wrapped up into finding that one piece that I could not see beyond it? Sure enough after becoming irritated, I decided to simply step away from it for a while. After returning to the puzzle the piece was discovered right away, as it had been in front of me the whole time! Sometimes we just need to step away from similar situations in life; in order to see them more clearly.

Perhaps those puzzle pieces could very well represent various things in life. Those "pieces" in life could represent: family, friends, events, milestones and celebrations. Life is just one big puzzle if you think about it in these terms:

1. Unless you are psychic then you are uninformed of how the final picture will look.
2. Initially all pieces are scattered and everyone is unique just like people.
3. You can start with the easy pieces or the harder ones.
4. Teaches you to practice patience over a period of time.
5. Take a time out as you will become frustrated.
6. Stop trying repeatedly to fit a piece into an opening that you know is never going to fit.
7. Perhaps you need to separate from a piece, move on to another, and then come back when you can see more clearly.
8. Utilizing another set of eyes belonging to a friend may prove to showcase their skills and techniques to teach you another way of solving a "problem".
9. Never give up… Your completed puzzle may be just around the corner!

I believe Marilyn Monroe said it best, *"I believe that everything happens for a reason. People change so that you can learn to let go, things go wrong so that you appreciate them when they're right, you believe lies so you eventually learn to trust no one but yourself, and sometimes good things fall apart so better things can fall together."* Each experience, whether good or bad, signifies a piece of the puzzle. If you were to remove one piece it would disturb the entire harmony of the ultimate outcome. Please understand and believe that some of your past pieces in life are far from pleasant and many bring despair and depression. As unimportant as they may or may not appear they bring you one more step closer to healing. When we are so hard on ourselves due to certain experiences we are far from healing and our growth is stifled. If you do not allow yourself to heal then nothing you do will ever become good enough.

Below are some reasons and behaviors to eliminate, while embracing the solutions suggested:

1. **You MUST be willing to forgive:** When you have slip-ups (and we all do) and can't forgive yourself, you stay  trapped. If you continuously harp on the should-haves, would-haves and could-haves, you can't move forward. Please be kind to yourself first and be sure to forgive yourself when you make a mistake. There are lessons to be learned at every turn so learn the lesson, and move forward not back.

2. **DO NOT compare yourself:** Do you find yourself attempting to "Keep up with the Joneses"? As a result, this comparison is a blow to your spirit and ultimately will kill any chance of happiness. Please understand that YOU are

155

unique, and this was no coincidence. There is only ONE you and no other was created on this planet. If you must compare, then please compare yourself to only yourself. I know this sounds strange but there will always be someone more attractive, wealthier or poorer, skinnier or larger, and greater or less than you are in certain areas. We can't go through life focusing on someone else; you must focus on your own journey.

3. **Perfection is only an illusion:** There is not ONE person who would claim to have it ALL. No one! Every one of us struggles with something. I personally struggle with my weight, for some it's financial, for some it's health concerns, others may have a mental illness, for some it's a sick parent, for some it's an discontented marriage, for some it's an addiction, for others it's a disturbed teen. Two people may externally look alike, but internally their situations are not the same let alone "perfect." Repeat after me, there is no such thing as perfect!

4. **Strive for excellence, NOT perfection:** Imagine you are running a marathon... little improvements cutting down your time each day is what keeps you motivated and moving. Or maybe the marathon was a bit much so imagine painting a picture... every day a new color is added to the easel, bringing you one step closer to the finished product and therefore a sense of accomplishment. Imagine applying for your dream job. There may be ONE ideal job in your mind, but that doesn't mean that your current work won't be fulfilling and give you a tremendous sense of happiness. Strive for excellence, not perfection as you will not be disappointed!

5. <u>**Celebrate all your victories no matter how big or small:**</u> Earlier this year I joined Weight Watchers to lose weight. Just today I celebrated losing 21 pounds! Why is it we only break open the champagne at the larger goals? Why not every 5 pounds, celebrate your mini milestones? Life is truly a journey and not a destination, so enjoy the ride! As you get closer to your final goals be sure to celebrate those small victories; as without those small victories there could be no BIG victory!

Do you practice self-compassion? If not, this could be another reason you may be experiencing self-inflicted pain and stress in your life. Are you spending enormous amounts of time assisting everyone else while ignoring yourself and self-compassion? Don't get me wrong, life is unquestionably about helping people, at the same time, we must not overlook that the greatest service we can ever award humanity is our own happiness, wholeness... and ultimately our own self-compassion! Let me aid you in acquiring the below strategies so that you are better equipped to help someone else:

Velcro Your Brain: I once read somewhere that your brain is like Velcro for negative experiences. The negative ones have a tendency to attach themselves like Velcro, and the opposite for Teflon exhibiting the positive experiences which we allow to glide away from our attention. By paying attention to the positive and joyful experiences, you can teach your brain to fasten itself to the good in life.

Alert to Our Feelings: As stated above, you are not how you feel! They do not define you, they run through you. As we have experienced, the brain enjoys building on those feelings and "creating" a tale such as "I have no control over my life." Be mindful to distinguish right then what is playing out is nothing more than a common pattern or a default response.

Choices are Options: Do not reject any of your emotions. Instead, detect them and willfully choose how you want to respond, not just react! Taking deep breaths grant you an opportunity to calm your physical and mental being in order to view your situation in a new way. Simply examine the emotion, experience it, and choose your response. How good will you feel now?

Adopt Self-Compassion: Decide and declare that it is time for you to be pleasant and loving to yourself. Those who adopt self-compassion are known to feel more joy, confidence, happiness and less stress, pain, depression, and F.E.A.R of failure.

A victorious woman is not perfect, but she is perfected through her faith. You are a victorious woman, and I encourage you to go forth and walk in your faith. Know and trust that all the pieces you need are there and that it is only a matter of time before they fall into place. Remembering that there is a big picture, a plan for everyone, and yes a plan for YOU! Your past playbook is void (because I said so) ☺ and now you have a chance to play a new game; a better game, a more successful game to create the extraordinary life you deserve. Since the clock is running and you are unable to get time back, make the most of today. Yesterday is history. Tomorrow is a mystery. Today is a gift. That's why it is called the present. It's a WRAP; you are uniquely GIFTED, so accept your PRESENT and focus on it TODAY as I DECLARE & DECREE YOU ARE INDEED AN UNSTOPPABLE WOMAN!

 Katia Steilemann, born and educated in Brazil, has recently dared to leave the stable well-paying corporate world and found her own consulting company, called Elyts Ltd. She combines the elements of leadership development, image consulting and interior design, offering a pioneer three-dimensional approach to help unfold a woman's full potential to live a more successful life.

An example for her unrelenting pursuit of innovation and style is a newly developed and self-designed product called Grabling — contemporary jewelry and stylish accessories, "bling" so-to-speak, that can be "grabbed" by infants and played with, allowing mothers and grandmothers to be fashionable whilst being themselves around their little ones and caring for them in a worry-free and empowered way.

Having worked for one of the largest multi-national, pharmaceutical, and chemical corporations for more than 13 years, 8 of them in Human Resources, gives her the great advantage to fully understand what businesses and leaders really need and therefore offer better consulting solutions.

Her latest achievement was to become a qualified Feng Shui expert certified by a Master in Hong Kong, and get specialized in Interior Design by obtaining a diploma from The Interior Design Academy in Australia. In recent years Katia has had the opportunity to reveal her artwork in more than twelve exhibitions, winning a number of prizes, including most recently an IBB Award, sponsored by the Brazilian Art Academy and the City of Sao Paulo, in commemoration of the city's 450 Years Anniversary.

Contact information:
www.elyts.biz
www.elytsbiz.wordpress.com
katia@elyts.biz

Chapter 13
Creating Rapport with Other Women
by: Katia Steilemann

Rapport is the connection between two people. The unspoken words that say "we are on the same page."

Almost every woman I talk with confirms that there is an unspoken difficulty to build a relationship and even trust with other women. Not many are willing to say it out loud and even fewer are ready to admit that they treat the same sex with mistrust, envy and caution.

While I was responsible for building mentoring relationships in a company, one of the big challenges was to find senior female executives willing to mentor other women. The few that made it up the hierarchical level would say with no shame that the mentees should learn it the hard way, just like they did. They didn't have the luxury of a mentor and that is what made them so great today.

Unfortunately, the same women are missing a big chance to help their company thrive economically, in diversity, and at the same time missing the opportunity to reevaluate their own leadership style. They might think they are great because they came so far, but what they don't see is that they have become same-sex predators. I don't mean to generalize this because I also know a few excellent female leaders out there that are willing to develop new talents, excel at networking, and do great in teamwork activities.

More and more you read blogs and e-discussions about the female rivalry topic at work. You come across comments like, "I prefer having a male boss because he is more objective and less

> "I prefer having a male boss because he is more objective and less emotional."

emotional," or "my female colleague hides important facts just to make me look incompetent," or "I don't want to be interviewed by a female manager because she will be much too picky," or "we can't seem to find common ground for a nice conversation," and so on.

Last week when I attended a lunch with both working and stay-at-home mothers, I realized how fragile the female friendship is. What seemed initially to be a very well connected group of women sharing common interests turned out to be a gathering of cordial females seeking opportunities to let out their poisonous comments about other members of the group that were not present. I think it took sixty minutes for the first ugly comment to be said and afterwards, everyone took a turn at being bitchy.

Dear girlfriends, sorry about these harsh words but I can't find another way to describe the event.

If you ever found yourself in the situation of having to make friends with other women because you either moved to a new city, changed jobs, or were left without friends after breaking up a long relationship, you will know how hard it really is to build rapport with other women. Don't you ever wonder why?

Mostly, it's not making the first contact, or being invited to the first party that is hard, it's what happens after that. You will find that women who share long years of friendships will hardly let you into their little group. You are welcome but you are not. Very beautiful women will rarely take another beautiful woman as a best friend. This is not new. There are plenty of movies that portray the social "unkindness" of women towards others. They get dominant over weaker females and repulsive against stronger opponents.

Some years ago, I was working in the same company as a personal friend of mine. We knew each other since childhood and used to meet on the weekends. We had, what I thought, a good connection. Around the second year at work I noticed she started to avoid me. She would not answer my emails or phone calls. And when she passed by me, she had a different look in her face and very often would look away. This really intrigued me. "Did I do something wrong?" If it had been somebody else I probably wouldn't have cared so much because I can't please everyone around me, but she was different. I missed her friendship and would do anything to figure out what I had done and how I could change it. So finally, after many attempts of talking to her I jumped into the same elevator and we had a moment for ourselves where she could not escape. I went directly to the point and asked what I had done to her. She invited me for a walk to talk. That is when, to my surprise, I heard what I never thought I would hear from a friend. She said she could no longer be friends with me because I make her feel less and diminished. I would outshine her and she felt envious of my life and achievements. My optimism and energy for life would make her feel like she is negative and lame. My looks made her feel like she needed to constantly improve hers (and let's note here that she is a beautiful blond, perfect body type of girl whose looks I envied!).

I was shocked... but I was also relieved and deeply grateful. Only a friend would say this out so clearly; feelings that are so ugly and weak. She said there is nothing I could do because I would have to stop being me. So the only thing left for me to do was to accept the fact that she would leave my life and hope that someday she realizes how cowardly it is to surrender to such thoughts and feelings. I still miss her friendship after more than ten years.

It just feels like a jungle out there. So what is the reason for us to behave like this? Do we have an ancient instinct that makes us build up such defenses? What do we gain from this behavior? Most importantly, how can we change?

I could not find any studies that bring a good conclusion and explanation to the social behavior patterns of women in regards to building rapport. Stumbled upon a few articles about mammals, but just thought it would go too far for the purpose of this chapter. The fact is that we need help in regaining our self-esteem and putting envy aside in order to achieve a higher purpose; to pursue healthy relationships with others of the same kind.

If you watch closely, relationships between mothers and daughters are the most difficult and intriguing. I believe there is something we can learn from them. According to researcher Karen Fingerman, an assistant professor of human development and family studies in Pennsylvania State University, the mother-daughter relationship matures mostly during adult life and gets stronger with the years. The main reason is that they share the same interest...that of investing in family. There is a moment in a daughter's life when she realizes that the mother is just another woman with similar challenges and fears, and stops seeing her as the enemy, the competitor.

I believe this study gives us the first hint on what we need to do in order to build rapport:
   a. Finding common ground and similar interests
   b. Acknowledging the other woman for the unique individual that she is

I know it's easier said than done because there is always the aura of rivalry in the air. When a woman first sees another woman that appears to be successful, thousands of thoughts go through her mind in a second. Where did she buy those shoes? How does she keep so slim? Is she married? Does she have children? Is her husband good looking? Why is she so successful?

We are so surrounded with preconceptions, that it gets really hard to acknowledge the other woman for who she really is. We either project onto her what we would like her to be (e.g. our best friend, a mother that cares, etc.), or we are blinded by our cultural differences, third party opinions, and own interests.

It's time to learn and start understanding the great benefits that relationships, networks, and team spirit with other women can do for the success of a business and also personal lives. Go ahead and dare to tell her she looks good, congratulate her for the achievements and success, praise her courage!

From my experience, unfortunately most women treat other women badly and they are the worst in corporate world where power is more explicitly challenged. Instead of sticking together, they give in to emotions of jealousy, competition, and the need to mark their territory. Suddenly they incorporate very male characteristics. They transform themselves after tasting the glory of power; losing their innate intuition for caring, understanding and compassion. There is the general fear that if you show these characteristics you are weak and will be overruled by other more aggressive personalities.

"When you see someone who is successful, you are either intimidated by them, or inspired by them."

-Dr. Anthony Gantt

Now here is a myth: Think about Oprah Winfrey, one of the most powerful ladies on earth that conquered the world by listening to and helping other women. If you look at her team, you will see cooperation, fun and hard work. What about Angela Merkel, the first woman to become chancellor of

Germany? She was heavily criticized in the beginning, but with time won the respect of the world with her softer voice and quiet diplomacy. Rapport happens on many levels.

The image of the other woman is what we see first and that leads us to form an opinion about her. If you like it or not, the overall looks can cloud the observers mind and already prevent them from wanting to meet with one another.

Through her body language she will speak her first unspoken words. Small clues like the distance she stands from her counterpart, the movement of her arms and position of her legs give hints about what she is feeling.

The third level of rapport is speech; what she actually says. What she says and how she expresses her opinion will make a difference in how she will be perceived by others.

Once you have overcome the first hurdle you start sharing ideas, values, and begin finding out what you have in common with the other person.

> *Let your guard down once in a while without being afraid that the other party will judge you. You might be surprised.*

Suddenly the snob woman next door likes hiking, just like you. The entrepreneur that comes home late every day enjoys cooking, just like you. But it's not always the nice and pleasant things in life that get women to feel a bond, it's the painful experiences as well. You can make a friend for life if you find that she also had cancer, lost a husband or a child, went through infertility, infidelity, and so on. You have someone to confide in; someone who understands you. I believe that women heal emotionally much faster when they know and talk to other women who are in the "same boat." This does not mean that you should expose your troubles immediately on the first encounter.

Especially those living outside of their home country or amongst different cultures may come to think that the language barrier is responsible for the difficulty to build rapport, but it doesn't really play a big role. Studies have shown that rapport is built only 7% by the words you say, the content/ dialogue. 55% comes from your body language, and the rest by the *way* you say things, the tone of your voice. The only barrier with language is the risk of a major misunderstanding and you getting really disappointed with a problem that does not really exist.

The environment you are in also helps build rapport. This is one of the reasons why virtual meetings will never be able to achieve the same that is achieved by contact in person. The smell of the room, the temperature, the lighting and the objects around you will either help or hinder you from creating a good rapport. Imagine you walking into a cold room, the few windows on the outside walls have no curtains. There is a bar with one old bartender who is watching some news about the Iraq war on TV. In this room are two businesswomen you are meeting that you have connected with online in a social networking group for female entrepreneurs. How much effort do you think you will have to put into building rapport with these two ladies?

Now imagine the same situation in a different place, a warm place, full of happy people, happy-hour atmosphere, some candles, and good music playing in the background. You just feel the environment embracing you when you walk in. You feel supported by the space and therefore one step closer to the people around you.

In a nutshell, here are the key skills for building rapport:
- Clear your mind of any preconception you might have (e.g. women that have short hair are not feminine, women from

Arab countries are submissive and weak, stylish women are egoists, etc.)

- Pay attention to body language. Yours and the other person's. People give us many non-verbal clues. If the counterpart is closed and inaccessible you could be open and welcoming and might be able to connect (e.g. uncross your arms, smile, look the person in the eyes, etc.). Come with a positive attitude and thoughts

- Use the space surrounding you in your favor. Your physical position towards the other person will let them know if you are genuinely interested or not (e.g. if you give them your back it's clear that you don't feel like talking to them). Find out what the preferred side of someone is. It is popular belief that if they are right-handed they will keep their closest friends on their right side.(*1)

- Put yourself in the other person's shoes. Don't try to guess how they are feeling or what they are thinking, but really feel and think as if you were in their skin.

- Ask the right questions; the ones that will help you find common ground and interests. Why would you ask if she likes golfing if you hate it?

- Show empathy by being honest and genuine. Don't try to be someone you are not. This will only bring tension into the situation and you will not find common ground.

Common mistakes you can do when building rapport:
- Only talk about yourself
- Show no interest about others through body language and not asking any questions
- Come with pre-conceived ideas of the other person or their situation.
- Starting a conversation if you're thinking, "Why am I even here?" Honestly, in this case it's better if you just leave!

- Letting envious feelings dominate your thoughts and reflect in your behavior;
- Never initiate contact again after the first meeting (friendships and relations need to be nurtured by both parties. Don't wait for the other person to call or email you, go ahead and do it yourself!)
- Giving up too soon on establishing future meetings (if the other woman turns down your first invitation, don't assume it is because she does not like you):

You know that you have created rapport when time has flown by during the conversation and you didn't even notice it. At the end of all the research, personal experiences, and discussions with friends and colleagues, I have come to the conclusion that envy is the biggest enemy for females creating quality rapport with other women.

Research has shown that envy and pleasure go hand-in-hand. Dr. Hidehiko Takahashi of Tokyo Medical and Dental University in Japan led a study called "The Schadenfreude study (*2)". Schadenfreude is the German word for "pleasure derived from another's misfortune." They have found that envy is a feeling <u>like any other feeling of pain</u> that is triggered in our brain. Only with the misfortune of another person that we envy, can this pain be relieved and we get a sense of reward.

It is my belief that we can get addicted to this form of getting rewarded. If we are not conscious of our thoughts and feelings, we will constantly need to see someone else have a bad day. Interesting enough, it is much easier for women to make social comparisons with others of the same kind, making other women victims of their bad wishes.

There is enough scientific evidence proving that pain can also be purely psychological. So, if pain can be "created" by the mind, so can the pain of envy. Therefore, the key to stopping envy lies in our own hands. If we want, we can choose to change our thoughts, choose to be better women and help others above our egoistic self.

(*1) You can read more about body language and find out your best side in the book "You say tomato, I say shut up", by Janine Driver, Mariska van Aalst
(*2) Original research paper: When Your Gain Is My Pain and Your Pain Is My Gain: Neural Correlates of Envy and Schadenfreude is published in Science.

Emilie Shoop is a sought after coach, and owner of Shoop Training & Consulting. She has a passion for helping people and organizations realize their true potential by improving leadership, engagement, and team skills. Emilie's passion has shone through her various life experiences from an engineer, a manager, a director, and a sales consultant in a variety of settings such as large corporations, government institutions, and small organizations.

One of Emilie's pet peeves is unhappy people in the work place. It is her belief that everyone has an innate desire to do well, and it is this belief that drives her to reach out and impact others.

Fueled by her passion and enthusiasm, her presentations are fun, interactive, high energy, impactful and results-oriented. She is an out of the box thinker and uses her skills to lead towards astounding results. She provides clients, teams and organizations the skills and tools for leadership and professional excellence.

Shoop Training and Consulting's goal is to maximize performance by providing training and performance solutions. By incorporating the right combination of assessments, one-on-one and group training programs, Shoop Training & Consulting will custom fit a package of tools and services for companies of any size, need, or goal.

Contact information:
Shoop Training & Consulting
PO Box 192
Heyworth, IL 61745
www.shooptc.com
eshoop@shooptc.com
(309) 981-3686

Chapter 14
Building Your Emotional Intelligence
by: Emilie Shoop

There are a plethora of books, audios, videos, and training seminars available about Emotional Intelligence. It is one of my favorite topics to discuss because it is something you already use in every aspect of your life. Also it is something that you have the ability to improve upon and grow over time, and you will see dramatic results from that work.

The concept of Emotional Intelligence was popularized in 1996 by author Daniel Goleman in his bestselling book entitled "Emotional Intelligence." Through both brain and behavioral research, Goleman makes the case that rather than IQ or technical skills; Emotional Intelligence is a better predictor for success especially in leadership. What does that mean for you? It means that how you approach life and handle life's challenges dictates how successful you can be versus how book-smart you are.

The best part of Emotional Intelligence is that it is not fixed at birth! It can be developed and improved in all of us. To me, that's very exciting because YOU have control over your life and the power to be unstoppable. Emotional Intelligence involves four different factors in your life.

Self-awareness

Self-awareness is your focus. How focused and in-tune with what is going on with your life are you? Are you on auto-pilot and just going through the motions?

Or, are you actively present and recognizing the choices you are making each day?

Ways you can increase your self-awareness:
- The act of focusing on your awareness automatically increases your self-awareness.
- Pay attention to the moment at hand; try not to think about everything else going on in your life.
- Put down distractions (phone, laptop, paperwork, etc.).
- Limit multi-tasking.

Consequences of being unaware:
- Making many mistakes.
- Missing opportunities.
- Ineffective communication.
- Being reactive instead of proactive.

Self-management

Self-management is how you are handling life. Each time there is an event that requires a reaction from you, you have the opportunity to **Choose to Learn** or **Choose to Resist**. Most importantly, you need to know who you are. How do you approach life? Do you see obstacles as a way to grow? Or is every obstacle an opportunity to blame someone else?

Ways to improve your self-management:
- Understand the way things are; remove the meanings you are giving situations and accept them as is.
- Accept that you are in control of your life and the choices you make.
- Define your vision. What do you want in life? What do you stand for?
- Explore your personal life purpose. Why are you on this planet?

Consequences for poor self-management:
- Increased conflict and stress.
- Low self-esteem.
- Embarrassing situations end up bigger than they should have been.
- Others may not trust you.

Social-awareness
Social-awareness is how you see and react to others' feelings, needs and concerns. This also includes the ability to help others develop. How well can you put yourself in someone else's shoes? Are you tuned-in to how others feel in the moment? Or are you sufficiently self-aware to be socially aware?

Ways to improve your social-awareness:
- Increase personal communications with others and limit faceless interactions.
- Be open to others' points of view.
- Acknowledge the emotions of others.
- Listen carefully to others and think before you answer questions.

Consequences for poor social-awareness:
- Others will think you don't care or are insensitive.
- You may be seen as untrustworthy.
- Misunderstanding the situation at hand.
- Being disengaged from the climate of your environment.

Relationship Management
Relationship management is how you use the three previous skills to interact with others. How well you use these skills will help you create successful relationships. It is important to have many successful relationships in your life. How are you taking care of

others? Are you patient, open, and approachable? Do others trust and connect easily with you?

Ways to improve relationship management:
- Work on the first three skills (self-awareness, self-management, and social-awareness).
- Understand others' values.
- Recognize the need for change and support the change(s).
- Create and maintain collaboration networks.

Consequences of poor relationship management:
- Others will resist your suggestions for change.
- Ineffective feedback will be given.
- Conflicts may end relationships.
- Poor decision making.

LIVING EMOTIONALLY INTELLIGENT

Choosing to live your life Emotionally Intelligent is possible, but it takes practice. Every day we are given many opportunities to exercise our Emotional Intelligence. Each time there is a moment that presents a challenge and demands a response, you can improve your skills. Consciously or unconsciously, we respond to that event in a way that moves us toward learning or resisting.

Typical challenges in your day:
- The power went out and you overslept.
- Your child announces at breakfast that he has to bring in treats to school that day.
- Someone gives you negative feedback on your big project at work.
- There is a traffic jam and you are now late.

A positive response to the challenge means that you are focused and in-tune with what is going on, you take ownership of the situation at hand, you show empathy to others in the moment, and you take a proactive approach to a solution.

When you handle these events poorly, you choose to resist. Therefore, you are not focused on what is going on. You blame others for the situation at hand, you don't take others' emotions into account, and you just react.

An example: Loss of Connectivity

Consider this story: One night, a teenager was not following directions and his parents could not get him to focus on what they were asking him to do. They also have a toddler and were all on their way out to dinner. Like most teenagers, this teenager always has the need to be connected to his friends via his iPod touch. As the parents get the toddler wrestled into his coat, shoes and hat, the teenager is frantically getting in a few more messages with friends before they leave the house. It takes him 10 times longer than it should for a teenager to get his shoes on and get out the door. At this point, the parents are extremely frustrated with reminding the teenager that he was asked to get ready while trying to keep the toddler ready to go. Finally, the family goes out to dinner. Whew!

When the family comes home, the parents decide that they all need a break from internet connectivity and disconnect the home network. The teenager realizes what has happened, and this sends him ranting and raving. Immediately, he starts crying and pouting.

He is so upset, he can't even think straight. When he finally asks the parents what happened to the internet connectivity, they explain that it is because of his behavior earlier and they are tired of competing with his iPod for his attention when it is needed. Unfortunately, the teenager gets more and more worked up. He then tells the parents that his entire social life is over now because he can't get online. Mind you, he has a cell phone and could call someone if he needed to talk. Eventually, he gets so upset that he decides that he is going to walk somewhere; the parents have no idea where he was going at 10 p.m.!

What the parents wanted was for their son to ask "what will it take for you to reconnect the network?" Instead, it turned into a huge uproar. The reaction was not what the parents expected at all! But, always trying to find the teachable moments, it was a great opportunity for the parents to help the teenager with his Emotional Intelligence.

When you take a look at how this situation played out, you can see that the teenager chose to resist and not to learn.

- *Lack Focus* – he did not grasp the reality that it was purely temporary and that it was within his power to have the internet connectivity restored.
- *Blame Others* – the parents heard how horrible they were, how it was all their fault that he couldn't get online, and how he didn't do anything wrong by sitting online while the family was trying to leave.
- *Disregard Others* – when teenagers are upset, they can be very hurtful in their choice of words (I don't think I need to elaborate).
- *Reactive* – since the teenager was so upset, he couldn't think clearly enough to come up with solutions to the problem.

Had the teenager decided to exercise his Emotional Intelligence and learn from the situation, it would have gone something like this (from the teenager's point of view):

- *Focused* – the disconnection is temporary, I have other ways to communicate with my friends, there are other things I can do for entertainment.
- *Take Ownership* – my lack of response to my parents caused their frustration and therefore the disconnection.
- *Show Empathy* – it is frustrating to wait on others when I want to go somewhere, I should consider that when my family is asking me to get ready.
- *Proactive* – I wonder what I can do to get the connectivity restored. I will ask!

Again, I realize it is very easy to see areas for improvement when you are looking at toddlers and teenagers. But, does this remind you of any situations you have run into in your life? In your workplace? In volunteer meetings?

An example: A New Opportunity

Consider this story: For a large portion of my career, I was a Network Engineer. I love technology and learning about ways to make your job or life easier through technology. However, I had gotten to the point in my career where in order to advance, I either had to learn technology at the 0s and 1s level, or move into management. I had (and still have) no desire to expand my knowledge to the 0s and 1s level. My passion is working with people to improve their performance, so management was a natural choice. However, our team already had a manager. There were no other management openings in our organization, so that meant I would have to look outside to advance. Since I loved my team and the organization was a great place to work, leaving did not appeal to me.

Finally, I decided to confide in my manager and ask for his advice. We discussed the aspects about being a Network Engineer that I enjoyed and the aspects that were not fulfilling. It turns out he was at a crossroads as well. He, in fact, enjoyed being a Network Engineer more than a manager and was trying to figure out if he should look outside the organization as well. Wow. I took the opportunity to propose that we switch positions. If we worked it right, we could both be happy and not have to leave the organization.

It took a few months, but we were able to negotiate with and sell upper management on the idea. We made the switch, and were both very happy with the changes. Taking the positive path really worked out well for both of us.

- *Focused* – I realized what I was missing in my position and what I wanted to be happy.
- *Take Ownership* – it was important that I take charge of the desire for a change, and not just blame others for my lack of fulfillment in the workplace.
- *Show Empathy* – when discussing the situation with my manager, I was able to empathize with what it would mean for him to lose an employee from his team.
- *Proactive* – when the opportunity arose to offer to switch positions, I took it!

Do you have a story where you took the positive path? It is very rewarding to look back at a time that you used Emotional Intelligence and turned a challenge into a great situation.

An example: A Poor Performance

Consider this story: Considering my love of technology and my love of working with people, I took a position in IT sales with a small company. It gave me the opportunity to build relationships, find solutions for problems, and be rewarded for the amount of effort I put in. The position also gave me the opportunity to exercise my Emotional Intelligence.

When you have a sales position, it is all about the numbers. Unfortunately, my numbers were pretty low. The sales I enjoyed working on were large problems, took a long time to develop, and a long time to pay off. Those sales are great if you have a lot of smaller sales sustaining you, which I did not. At last, it was time for my manager to talk to me about it.

After the conversation, I felt beat up and worn out. (I could write a book on how the conversation could have been more productive on his part, but that's not the point here.) I was faced with the choice to learn or to resist. As tempting as it was to resist, I chose to learn.

- *Focused* – I had to separate the emotions I was feeling from the facts. It wasn't that I was a bad person, or a failure. My numbers were low because I had not concentrated on the right type of sales.
- *Take Ownership* – it was very easy to blame my manager for not training me as he promised he would, but that wasn't going to change anything. It was up to me to learn how to sell, and sell well.
- *Show Empathy* – although the conversation felt like an attack on me, I had to empathize with my manager and the owner of the company. The company was small and everyone needed to be contributing at a high level.
- *Proactive* – I started attending webinars, reading books, seeking motivation, and asking lots of questions to help

improve my sales. When my slump started, I started to recoil and not want to leave my cube. Now was the time for me to take charge and be active.

It was very tempting for me to take the path of resistance. In fact, I did take the path of resistance for as long as I could but it was not getting me anywhere. Choosing to learn was extremely satisfying. When have you been in a similar situation? What did you do?

Exercise
Now that you have seen some examples of Emotional Intelligence in action, let's take the opportunity to work on improving yours. Think of an opportunity or challenge you were faced with recently. It can be from work, home, friends, and so on.
Opportunity/Challenge:

_____

_____

Self-awareness – Did you add any meaning to the situation based on something else going on in your life? Or were you clearly focused on the situation at hand?

_____

_____

Self-management – did you **Choose to Learn** or **Choose to Resist**? List out each of the steps and how you handled them:

	choose to resist	choose to learn	
_____	Lack Focus	Focused	_____
_____	Blame Others	Take Ownership	_____
_____	Disregard Others	Show Empathy	_____
_____	Reactive	Proactive	_____

Social-awareness – were you others focused in this situation? What did you do to see an opportunity for someone else to grow in this situation?

_____

_____

Relationship management – was your interaction with others in this situation valuable to them? What did you do to increase their trust in you?

_____

_____

Remember that being aware is the first step to increasing your Emotional Intelligence. Thinking through times when you have been successful in learning from the challenge you were presented, and when you resisted the challenge, will help you improve for the next opportunity. Emotional Intelligence is not a place you arrive at, it is a journey and it takes work. Nobody handles every situation perfectly, but you will get better if you stop and think "how can I do that better next time?"

Colleen Lindberg is a passionate entrepreneur, author, leader and enthusiastic business consultant and coach. She is the owner of the company C. Lindberg Consulting, an organization assisting companies and entrepreneurs to better understand themselves and their abilities, so that they can maximize their performance.

Getting what you want in life is so important. It is the fuel behind your talents and greatness. Igniting the greatness in others is something that Colleen values and believes in everyday.

Born in Winnipeg Manitoba, Colleen learned at a young age what entrepreneurship was all about. Starting her first company at the age of the 6, selling lemonade and organizing garage sales, she greatly learned what it would take to make it in this world if you were going to do something big. From there on the dream started to manifest.

Opening and running many types of businesses, Colleen got her love for the industry through her experience. She is a certified coach and Kolbe consultant, which allows her to teach others about their greatness, through their cognitive abilities and natural instincts. Her passion for creating team synergy connects her into all different industries, opening up doors for companies to have support and everyone working together.

Colleen is also a seminar speaker and is the author of the soon to be released book *"Change the Light Bulb, the mindset behind success."* Her passion to help people comes in many forms and she loves the journey of discovery. Do you know how great you are?

Contact information:
C. Lindberg Consulting
www.clindbergconsulting.com
colleen@clindbergconsutling.com
905-505-2249
Toronto, Ontario

Chapter 15

R.E.S.P.E.C.T. – Setting Boundaries & Speaking Up for Yourself
by: Colleen Lindberg

Like the great Aretha Franklin belted out in her famous song "R-E-S-P-E-C-T find out what it means to me", leaving women everywhere singing it in their kitchens and dancing up storms on the dance floor. What does this line mean to you?

If you were like me growing up, I was taught through the examples of the women role models in my life, that women were not to speak up for what they believed in. They were supposed to "suck it up" and keep their opinions to themselves. Can you relate to this? Through much exploration, I came to realize that part of life, relationships, and business is sticking up for yourself and setting boundaries/limitations so people don't walk all over you. Who are you if you aren't living your purpose? Are you just a fly on the wall watching as things pass you by? Do you believe that you and I were just put here on earth to be walked on? I don't think so. We are all made for greatness. We are all here to accomplish this great

Who are you, really, if you aren't standing in your personal power?

task on earth. It's something bigger than us; bigger than we can even imagine it to be. Expressing who you really are is the first piece to getting and discovering your greatness. So, are you living in your personal greatness? Speaking up for what you want, in all avenues, is the key to starting to get this. Let me assist you with this acronym so you will always remember to live in R.E.S.P.E.C.T. for yourself.

R- Realign Personal Objectives

You are important and it's time for you to remember that. Creating a game plan for your goals and where you want to go is an important part of setting boundaries in your life. Without knowing what you want, how can you set boundaries around it? How do we get to this place of Personal Objectives? Start by answering these questions:

1) What is important to you?
2) If you were to make a list of the things that you're responsible for (kids, career, partner, friends, family, etc.), what would be your number one priority? How would you rate them in order of importance? (Please be honest with yourself. I have watched many people number certain things near the top of the list because they believe that they <u>have</u> to, or should do it, not truly  honoring what's important to them.) Sometimes as parents we feel that we should put our kids above everything else. Please sit with your answers and make sure that they are true to the authentic you.
3) From that list, what takes priority in your life over everything else?
4) Are the top 3 things something that you focus on in your everyday life? If not, why? (This question alone will bring up some emotion for you).

So the real question is, "What boundaries need to be set up in order for you to be living in that priority every day?" The

185

whole point of this chapter is for you to be able to see what is important to you, and for you to be consistently getting that in your life every day.

You are important and the things that are important to you matter. Reminding yourself of this is equally significant. Some of us have been conditioned to think that what we want is not of value or should be considered last over everyone else in our life. Can you relate to this? If so, it won't be an easy task for you to remind yourself that you are worthy of getting everything that you want in life. It might take months of telling yourself that you are worth it and that you have value. Do it anyway. Write it down for yourself and put it somewhere where you will see it every day. "WHAT I WANT MATTERS!"

E - Exercise your voice

There is a reason why we have the ability to talk and to think. The reason is so we can use our vocal chords to verbally express what's on our minds. It's not like some people have a voice and others don't. We all have the same opportunity to speak up for what we want, or say what we think and feel. Have you been doing this lately? If not, let's think about why. Maybe...

- You don't think you are smart enough and don't want to say something stupid
- You were taught that women don't have anything relevant to say
- You don't think that you or what you have to say are important enough
- It's because you don't have the belief in yourself and you thought that it was ok for you to remain in silence, because it didn't really matter anyway.

Whatever the case may be for you, the only way that you will absolutely be able to move forward in life is by knowing that you have a voice, then speaking what's important to you.

How do you start doing this? One little step at a time. If this is a challenge for you, I can absolutely relate to that. There was also a time in my life where I thought my opinion didn't matter. It took me a long time to realize that my opinion *did* matter. To whom did it really matter? Me. The only person that we have to prove anything to is ourselves. Whether you are wrong in the answer or feel awkward in voicing your opinion, I encourage you to do so. Start standing up for yourself. Don't allow others to put all their opinions on you, when you also have your own voice. It's time to start speaking.

S - Stand in Belief

Stand in the belief that things will get easier. Better said than done, right? It's not easy to change a habit, let alone a belief system. For you, it might have been years since you've really stood up for what you believed or set boundaries around what you wanted. Maybe looking back, you've never done it at all. That could be the fear that you've been holding on to; the fear of: the unknown, failure, success and even the fear of true happiness. The definition of *fear* and *faith* surround the same principle: *to believe in something unknown.* We can have fear or we can have faith in something; both are equally possible. So why not choose the latter and stand in the belief that things can change? Once you do this, there will be many more rewards and gifts for you to acknowledge in your life.

Maybe you have experienced this before and maybe you have had a sense that it could happen to you. Why not just try it and see what happens…what do you really have to lose? Imagine the feelings of gratitude and sense of purpose overwhelming you and the feeling that you are on the right path, at the right time, enjoying the journey. The only way these feelings can manifest is through the belief that they can come true. What do you believe?

P - Personal Power

What does this really mean? You, my friend, have a personal power plug or an on/off switch. It's the switch that allows you to go for what you want and get the things that are important to you. It's the "I won't take any crap from anybody" switch. Some of us have been taught that it's rude to have this type of mind-set. I agree to an extent. What if you could have respect for yourself and get everything you want, without having a sense of entitlement? That is what I am talking about. It's not the negative, "you owe me attitude", it's the "I'm worth respect and know where I am headed" attitude.

Personal power is standing in your great gifts and talents. It's making choices that reflect the beauty inside of you and your beliefs. It's about having a voice and a story that is to be shared. It's about knowing that you are perfect just the way you are and it's time that you shared that with the world. That is what personal power represents. How do you get there? It all starts with what you think about yourself. Here is an exercise that will help guide you through this process:

"The Woman in the Mirror" Exercise

Every morning and every night before you go to sleep I want you to look at yourself in the mirror. Look at yourself directly in the eyes and say to yourself:

1) I am proud of you
2) I love you

3) I appreciate you
4) I believe in you
5) I forgive you
6) I am doing the best that I can with the knowledge, skills and understanding that I have.

This exercise will help shift the mindset that you have about yourself. It will remind that you are a woman, and it will enable you to realize that you are deserving of everything that you want to receive in your life. It's a powerful exercise and one that might shake you to the core. Some people don't feel anything for weeks, keep on the path and know that subconsciously you are making a difference. It did for me... let's see what it does for you!!

E - Eliminate the "should" and the "have to"

"You should do this..." "You have to do that..."

Blah, blah, blah... Have you heard this before? People "shoulding" all over you. There are many people in our lives who want to tell you what you "should be" or "have to be" doing with your life, even though they have your best interest at heart. They are the ones who are quick on the advice, even when you haven't asked them for it!

Do you know people like this? Sometimes it's even the people in our lives we least expect to be like this. They mean well... they really do (well most of them do). What if you were to set up a boundary with them and say, "I appreciate your enthusiasm for my life, however I will handle this one on my own. If I make a mistake, then so be it. Agreed?"

This life that you are living is meant for you to live; you are here to learn and grow as an individual. Unfortunately, if you listen to what everyone else thinks you "should be doing" or what they think you "have to do", then where is the real personal explorations and growth?

There was an exercise I did once where I decided to take all the "shoulds" and "have tos" out of my life. I thought, "If I don't like people saying it to me, then I want to make sure I'm not saying it to others." I decided to eliminate the "should's" from my own vocabulary. It was very challenging at first, but it got easier. Try it for yourself so you will know. After a few weeks, it became very rewarding. It was a sense of self-satisfaction to know that I wasn't trying to tell other people what they "should" or "have to" do. I brought in some friends and family for reinforcement to make me aware of when I said it; even to this day. You are the only one in your life that SHOULD be telling yourself what to do!

C - Consistency

There is one common behavior human beings share. We start off really strong, dedicated, and excited about something, and then somewhere along the way we let our guard down and lose the push to keep at it. This task that was once so important, we now find ourselves asking, "ahh… did it really matter anyway?" Yes, it matters and setting boundaries in your life and sticking to them is a very important thing. It dictates the threshold and your self-respect, for others and not only that, for yourself as well. If people in your life know that after a week things will go back to the way they were, what kind of change are you enforcing? None. I have heard it time and time again, "Oh, don't worry mom will forget in a few days and we will be able to get what we want," or "If we bug her enough, she will cave in," or "She is saying 'no' for now, but I can change that." And I am sure there are many more examples.

Here is an example that a friend of mine set in her life. She is a single mom and was dating a man that she really liked. He was insistent on sleeping over at her place, however she did not want

her son to wake up in the morning and see him there. So she set the boundary with her new found partner. She said, "I have no problem with you staying over as long as you are not here when my son wakes up in the morning." He agreed and she held him accountable to that boundary. There was a morning where the man had to hide in the bathroom because the alarm didn't go off and her son was awake. She left, drove her son to school and then he was allowed out of the bathroom. She warned him in the beginning that it's about boundaries and limitations. What boundaries have you set lately and not upheld? Are there some boundaries in your life now that you might want to revisit?

T - The Time is Now

Maybe you are thinking to yourself, "Well it's too late. I am too old to be setting boundaries. I have been in this relationship for 35 years, so why would things change now?" The mentality of human beings is that there is only a certain amount of time that we have to get things accomplished, which is true in many circumstances. However, when it comes to taking action and taking charge of our life, there is no limit. The present is the best time to start. It doesn't matter whether you are 16 or 76, change can happen at any age. If you are thinking that this could be challenging, this might not work, or wondering what these people are going to think when I do this, then stop! You are engaging in self-sabotage. I have been there; I know what it will take to go through the change. I know the feelings that you will encounter and some of the resistance that you might have. I also know that once you start to do this, you will be able to see major changes not only in your life, but also in the lives of those around you. It's never too late to start standing up for yourself; in fact this is absolutely the perfect moment for you to do this… you know why? Because you are finally ready to stand in it. That's why.

It only takes one person to raise the bar, for others to want to raise their bars higher as well. It's time that we as parents start to be the real examples for our kids, to show them that self respect is above all else the important foundation in anything we do. It's time for us as people to ignite respect in our environments, workplaces and families. It's time for the world and all the people in it, to actually stand in who they are, what they want and start to make a difference first in themselves, and then in the lives of others. That is really the goal… to ignite your greatness so that you can go out and ignite the greatness in others. How can you possibly fulfill your purpose in life if you're not being who you are? It's time for you to stand up for yourself and truly, get the life you want. I look forward to hearing about your great journey!

Deborah Clark is a Speaker, Author, Facilitator, and Mentor. After many years working as an Administrative Assistant she became involved with Toastmasters International. She has held several officer positions as she progressed through the learning modules. She continues to mentor new corporate clubs, train new members, and judge speech competitions. Deborah eventually presented workshops for the Toastmasters district conferences, professional associations, non-profit, and adult school/continuing education programs.

As a niche professional speaker, Deborah knows how to deliver programs that provide value to audiences. She provides training development and feedback to attendees that they can utilize immediately. She is also a member of the Fine Speakers Bureau. She is an experienced facilitator who can make audiences comfortable while sharing valuable information. Her background includes all aspects of meeting development, and event organization. She works one-on-one with clients to identify their needs for a successful presentation.

Deborah is a contributing author for two books that were published this year: Life Choices Navigating Difficult Paths, and Life Choices Putting the Pieces Together. Participation in the Unstoppable Woman's Library is another opportunity for Deborah to expand her writing experience. She looks forward to sharing her life experiences in hopes that it will empower every woman who reads it.

Contact information:
P O Box 2214
Bloomfield, New Jersey 07003
973-991-1726 (w)
973-735-4994 (c)
http://dclark6581.com

Chapter 16

Having the Courage to be Courageous-
Are You Ready?
by: Deborah D. Clark

Wouldn't it be great if we could take every opportunity that comes our way, and put it somewhere until we are ready. It's like when the kids call you, "wait a minute." Or when the phone rings, "wait a minute." Opportunities are the doors to the decisions we make that affect our lives. We as women are always waiting for the right time, the best time, or when we are ready to address it, open it, use it, share it, or show it to everybody else. How many times do we pack away stuff until the time is right, until the day arrives, or until we just can't take it anymore; even if we aren't necessarily ready? Let's take a minute to talk about having courage and what it means to say, "Now I'm Ready".

If you suffer from anxiety and fear it can become easy to believe you are the only one. It is common for individuals to believe no one really understands. I think these statistics may provide hope in knowing you are not alone.

Anxiety Disorders
Anxiety disorders include: panic disorder, obsessive-compulsive disorder, post-traumatic stress disorder, generalized anxiety disorder, and phobias (social phobia, agoraphobia, and specific phobia). The following statistics are provided by the National Institute on Health as per;
http://www.fearofstuff.com/headline/putting-statistics-to-fear/

- Approximately 40 million American adults ages 18 and older, or about 18.1 percent of people in this age group in a given year, have an anxiety disorder.
- Anxiety disorders frequently co-occur with depressive disorders or substance abuse.
- Most people with one anxiety disorder also have another anxiety disorder. Nearly three-quarters of those with an anxiety disorder will have their first episode by age 21.

What are you doing?

You need tools to evaluate your current life position in relationship to the life you are living. Are you doing what you think you are doing, or are you really not doing anything at all? All you know is that you're not ready.

Tory Johnson an award-winning business leader, national network television contributor, popular speaker and bestselling author; recently interviewed mega bestselling author, Daniel Pink, about his most recent book, "DRIVE: The Surprising Truth About What Motivates Us."

There's a neat anecdote he shared that I want to share with you.
Dan Pink suggests asking yourself, "what's my sentence?" In other words, how can you summarize the mission of your work clearly and concisely?

The second question Pink suggests asking yourself every night, "was today better than yesterday?"

An Oprah Book Club selection *A New Earth* by Eckhart Tolle has the tools to guide you to a spiritual transformation.
http://www.oprah.com/oprahsbookclub/A-New-Earth-Are-You-Ready-to-be-Awakened

The Free Management Library offers free on-line Various Self-Assessments for Personal and Professional Development: http://managementhelp.org/personaldevelopment/self-assessments.htm

Journals are very helpful in finding out what's going on with you. If you don't see what you are doing, then you don't know what to do. The journal is a great tool. You need to write it down, read it back, figure it out, or celebrate it. Who knows you could be doing better than you think.

Book Factory is a leading journal manufacturer and offers a variety of fine quality journals in many types, styles and formats. Customization and personalization are available for all of our books. Add your logo or artwork to the cover or pages to create a custom journal.

Barnes and Nobles offers leather journals, decorative journals, inspirational journals, and specialty journals. Some of you may already have a journal or other means of expressing your challenges. In those cases the evaluation is not necessary, but a review may still be in order. Have you established a goal, with a timetable, or an objective? Are you getting the things done that you want to get done?

How are you doing it?

I admit there is nothing new in keeping a journal; in fact blogging is far more popular these days. According to Wikipedia, as of February 16, 2011, there were over 156 million public blogs in existence.

Most blogs are interactive, allowing visitors to leave comments and even message each other via widgets on the blogs and it is this interactivity that distinguishes them from other static websites.

I would imagine that the pressure of having comments from other individuals on your progress or failure can be quite daunting. The journal on the other hand is private, and you can beat yourself up at will in your own time, but at a minimum always. The point is, you have a record of your journey.

The first journal, (blog if you prefer), is the best. The first time you read who you are is so enriching. You can be inspired to new heights or devastated to realize that you haven't done any of the things you wanted to do. Please don't be alarmed. You have to acknowledge the situation for what it is, good or bad. This is the start of the beginning. This is how you figure what you need to get ready. This is where all the stuff is. This is why you have the journal. Often, even in the worst case scenario people will continue to proclaim, "I'm ok", (no you're not). I am sure you have seen at one time or another someone who is a total wreck. Their life is in shambles, but they continue to pretend they have it all together, when in fact they are so "Not Ready". If you can't honestly accept your life the way it really is, you will never have a better one. If you do not want to improve yourself, you will always be where you are now. Is that really working for you?

I want you to be honest with yourself. I need you to be honest with yourself. You need to commit to yourself. When you read about all of the things you are doing, all the sacrifices you have made, what do you have? Think about all the opportunities around you that you don't see because you are so busy, doing WHAT?! Your time is precious. Your life is golden. Your future is what you want it to be. Now is when you will figure out what you want it to be. Be outrageous, be abundant, be determined, and be alive. Yes, you are alive, I hear you breathing. All of us do what we need to do. All of us get it done. I think we need to give ourselves more credit for making it work. Now you need to give yourself the tools to make it work for you. I have no idea what you want to be when you grow up. Remember that question? That question is the number one childhood dilemma. The question asked by every aunt, every uncle, grandparent, teacher, baby sitter, even strangers on the street. Tell me, why was it not ok to just say. "I don't know"? It was not ok because as children we were expected to have a plan, or at least a dream. Fortunately, adulthood responsibilities gave us plenty of excuses for not getting it done. How convenient is that?! Well people, the excuse hall pass has expired. You are to report to the rest of your life ASAP!

Whatever is not working let it go. If it is working, enhance it; see what else you can do with it. Many of you are probably half way there. I would venture to say most of you are in a much better place than you thought, and when you see it in writing you will be very surprised. That is a very cool thing. Enjoy it. If you read your journal entries and start thinking, "This is not good," that is why you wrote it down. If you think it's not so good, then it probably isn't. No problem, you can fix it. You are going to take a long hard look at why you think it's not good, and you will clear some space, and work it out. You can do this, you will try, and you will succeed. Break the mood with a funny story about something that happened to you. Humor always helps.

Do Something Different

I hate self help books. If I could help myself, I wouldn't need a book. What I do like is guidance. If a book can give me tools I can use, I like that. I hope some of the publications recommended earlier are helpful tools that will guide you to success. I know there will be some of you who will say that you have tried so many times to make life changes and have not been able to get it done. If you are one of those people, I will say this to you, TRY AGAIN!

If you are truly, stuck, then you may want to consider counseling. Sometimes we need to talk to someone, a real person who will listen and offer tools that we can use. Perhaps the book thing does not work for you. Be honest. Consider all the options, especially ones you haven't tried yet. Seriously, there is no way you have tried absolutely everything.

AT WORK: Refer to your Employee Assistance Plan. Most company EAP plans provide mental health counseling for stress, depression, loss of loved ones, in a private confidential setting. Then you can read the book.

OUTSIDE OF WORK: The American Mental Health Counselors Association offers a national on-line counselor search option by state and city.

COMMUNITY: Most communities have a mental health resource center available. Check with your local hospital. Sometimes a group session is just what you need.

I am a strong advocate of counseling services. I have used both an EAP and private services at different times in my life. It is a far better thing to say "I need help", than to not say it at all. One of the things I learned through counseling is how to identify the habits that were creating the stress for me. I had to learn to say no, and not feel guilty about it. I would arrive at my session a total wreck, exhausted, and drained. I would then proceed to cry like a baby for thirty minutes, (which is quite refreshing actually), play the victim of all my complaints. At one point I was in therapy continuously for over a year before I figured it out. It really clicked for me when I was right back in six months for the exact same issues. Bad Habits are hard to break, so don't be discouraged if it takes a while to come together for you. Until you clear your head you can't think straight, and you certainly can't start any kind of personal evaluation. The personal evaluation, (journal, blog) is the first step to your path to being the best person you can be.

One more hint about counseling, it is probably not a good idea to go to a session, cup your head in your hands and say anything about hearing voices, feeling like your brains are going to explode, or that you can't take it anymore. Trust me, not a good look. You may find yourself backtracking fast to avoid an admission for an in-patient psychiatric evaluation. You just need a little guidance, you are not a raving maniac. Go to your session prepared to list your complaints clearly and accurately. Examples:

- I need to learn to identify my stress factors.
- I am feeling very overwhelmed, how did I get here?
- I am always trying to please people, what makes me do that?

You want constructive feedback, so don't waste the appointment time complaining, or not making any sense. Consider therapy as a tool to help you manage your life. Once you manage your life, you can achieve your goals.

Don't Do This

I want to share a true story with you about what not to do with your stuff. Think about those boxes in the basement, the boxes in your mind that trigger the fear and doubt that cause you to say once again, "I'm not ready."

Many years ago I worked in the Physical Therapy Department of a large hospital. One of the out- patients was an older woman, (her names was Ms. Ann) who came in almost every day to ride the stationary bike all of twenty minutes. After she rode the bike she would sit in the reception area and chat with the rest of the patients (and anyone else who listened). Ms. Ann was the epitome of elegance and taste. She attracted attention when she walked into the room. All of her outfits were color coordinated. Her makeup was a little over done, but she was a beautiful woman. She had to use a cane to keep her balance. She liked big beaded necklaces with earrings to match. I think we all looked forward to seeing her each day. Whenever we asked her why she was dressed up, she would smile and reply, "you never know when you are going to meet your gentlemen friend." She amazed me with her confidence, and flair, especially since most of the time she looked better than me. She would sit in the reception area talking mostly to the men. She loved the attention. The men liked her too. One time she brought me a present. It was a pair of sparkling blue earrings with black lace trim, not quite my style, but cute. The gesture touched my heart. I wanted to be like her, I wanted her strength, her endurance, her ability to still believe. One day Ms. Ann did not show up. Later that day we found out she had been admitted in to the hospital. Ms. Ann had a stroke at home and was not doing well at all. She only came down for therapy once or twice during her admission. After several weeks, Patient Care Services began to make arrangements for Ms. Ann to be discharged. As part of the exit interview process a social worker visited her home. Ms. Ann lived in a rented room of a boarding house that was a renovated mansion. It was in a prestigious neighborhood with many huge older mansions that at one time were home to wealthy families. Her room was small and sparsely furnished with a bed and a small dresser. The rest of the room was filled with furniture crammed in corners, and boxes piled to the ceiling. There was just enough room to get to the bed, open the dresser draws, and hang clothes in the closet. All of her outfits were hung neatly with the jewelry pinned to the hangers in zip-lock plastic bags. The bed had silk pillows with fringe. The windows were concealed by the boxes, the only light came from a small lamp on the dresser. When the social worker asked Ms. Ann what was in the boxes she smiled and replied, "I have been saving these things for when I meet my gentleman friend. I want to be ready to set up house for him and me." Social Services deemed the room unsuitable for habitation. Ms. Ann was placed in a Senior Citizens Housing Complex across town. Some say when all of the boxes were unpacked she had enough to completely furnish her new one bedroom apartment. It was less than a year later that Ms. Ann died.

I believe Ms. Ann died of a broken heart. To unpack those boxes meant she had to face the realization that her gentlemen friend was not coming. She was confronted with being alone in her love nest; it was more than her heart could stand. I don't know what her last days were like. I don't know if she sat at her new kitchen table crying from loneliness, or if she just slowly lost her will to go on day by day until she finally lay down and passed away. What I will always remember is her smile, her grace, her undying love for a man she never met. She maintained such a deep devotion to her dream that it was the source of the light in her life. Do you love anything like that? You should; you should love yourself like that. Do you have the courage? Are you ready?

 Suzanne is an unstoppable entrepreneur often called the 'Spiritual Visionary.' She has a diverse professional background including being the Founder of OraOxygen Airport Spa, Letourneau & Associates, Lifestyle Centre and now, Passionicity, where "Passion connects with Purpose." Author of "Soar with Vulnerability", co-author of "Adventures in Manifesting – Health & Happiness," her quest to understand others and touch their hearts is her destiny in life. As a speaker and seminar leader, she travels worldwide offering her own insights to help you find your purpose.

Contact information:
www.passionicity.com
www.suzanneletourneau.com
suzanne@passionicity.com
1.888.364.3005

Chapter 17

Mending Wounded & Broken Spirits
by: Suzanne Letourneau

What is one to do when one loses its spirit, its passion and, its purpose in life?

For five long years I pretended that I was not hurt. I tried to convince myself that everything was okay. I covered the wounds and hid my vulnerability - the one thing I knew I could do very well. Perhaps you know exactly what I am talking about.

One day in 2009, while I was attending another supposedly *transformational* seminar, I found myself in front of a group of people with a microphone in my hand. How did that happened? I have no clue. In all the other seminars or conferences I've been to, I made sure I was making myself invisible when entering the room.

This time all I know is that it felt so familiar standing there, humble and defenseless, open and fearless, with this microphone in my hand. It was just like riding a bicycle. My whole being turned inwards and, I felt something happening.

For the first time in five excruciating years, I could actually feel something. ***Could something still be alive inside of me?***

Before I go on talking about what happened, losing my purpose and my passion, I feel it is important for you to know and understand where I come from. Why am I writing this chapter on wounds and broken spirit? And what makes me the expert on the subject?

We all have wounds to heal. Grief to endure and, at different times of our lives, a broken heart to glue back together. How do we pick ourselves up after each challenge and disappointment? In her book, *Heal Your Body*, by Louise Hay, she explains the connections between physical dis-eases and their underlying emotional blockages. These blockages are the result of mental thought patterns.

Where do thoughts come from and how are they controlling us? How do we become aware of our thoughts? How do we recognize a thought versus a feeling? By changing our thoughts we change the perspective of a situation. Therefore, a negative situation could instantly be changed into a positive one. One of my goals is to help you become aware of the thoughts as you are having them. As you do, you will have the opportunity to change your experiences. Which situation would you like to change right now?

My story is probably not that different than yours. The only difference perhaps, is that I decided to write about it. I realized that the only way to completely heal myself from all this pain is to share it.

So where do I come from? I am the middle child of a family of three girls from middle class working parents in Montreal, QC. Our family was a *dysfunctional* family. Does it sound familiar to you? I bet it does.

As all good dysfunctional family members, I created a *camouflage*. A camouflage that would protect me from the outside world. It would also protect me from the sad reality of my own tribe. Alcoholism, fights, fears, embarrassments and that constant *small voice*. You know the one I am talking about?

Do you remember a time where you felt you were on top of the world, because you had done so great? It could be because you were almost at the top of your class. Or that you got hired at this job which required three very challenging interviews. Or that you simply had created this wonderful drawing?

What if everything and every time you did something that had tremendous meaning for you, was never recognized or encouraged? What if your vision of you being anything you wanted to be in life, was discouraged by your parents through their fear base limitations?

Do you recognize any of these patterns for yourself? This was my reality. Each member of my *tribe* had created its own little imaginary world. Either it be through abuse of alcohol, drugs, work, emotional dependence, or simply from dreams. I have probably tried each one of these myself.

But mostly, my world has always been one of work and focus. Even when I was only twelve years old, I had this focus and determination. A determination to make my vision come through. Even though my vision was not completely clear, I knew I wanted to make a positive difference in people's lives. I knew I wanted to make a difference in my own life. I wanted to live without limitations or fear. I wanted to live without any baggage. I sought to live without blame and resentment. Quite a task wouldn't you say?

After multiple jobs, a couple of careers, hard work and many disappointments, I had finally created my ideal life and was living my soul's purpose.

I had created, founded and, opened the first Oxygen Wellness Airport Spa in the world – OraOxygen. It had a **Mission** - to redesign the experience for the traveler at the airport. And it had a **Vision** – to be located in all major hub airports in the world. I had found my life's purpose.

To all unstoppable women *entrepreneurs* out there, I know you know what I am talking about. To all of the unstoppable *women* out there, I have no doubt that you will replace your undesirable job with something that you have been striving for all of your life. To all unstoppable *mothers* out there, I trust that you will open your hearts to the beauty of giving birth to the realization of your dream. For you, it might have been a child. For me, it was my self-created company.

Whatever it is, a business, a foundation, a child, a teaching, etc., you know when you have found your life's purpose. And I had.

I am writing this chapter on wounds and broken spirits because my life's purpose was abruptly and unexpectedly taken away from me, just shortly after getting it. That's right! I lost my company, the business I had created, *my baby* - to the acquisitive hands of my investors. Who could ever imagine, that a life's purpose could be stolen away from you?

Well, it happened to me and for five tormenting years, I thought I was dead inside my body. My body was moving, yes, but everything else was numb. I did everything I could to get out of this *numbness*. Every time I thought I had finally found the way, I found myself right back into it.

Until one day, when something *magical* happened. I say *magical*, because I never thought that my *rebirth* was going to come from this unforeseen source - a source that you and I both have. A source we all have. We just need to reconnect to it. And this is what I want to share with you.

My sharing is coming to you under the form of simple, but profound exercises and insights. Insights that worked for me and I have no doubt will work for you.

Insights that will open the door to who you really are. When you do, you will realize that all is connected. *We* are all connected. My goal is to take you to that space. To the space where all wounds are healed. Where spirits are reunited and where vulnerability and authenticity are chiefs of the *tribes*. This unforeseen and magical source is our *vulnerability*

Your vulnerability is your biggest gift.

In this exercise, I share the 5 easy steps to embrace your vulnerability.

1. **First, you need to STOP and <u>be</u> with the pain.**

   - Where is the pain? Is it in your body? If so, which part of the body?
   - Is it in your heart? Do you feel your heart tighter or smaller? Do you feel your heart ready to burst?

208

- Is it in your mind? Do you feel stressed and tensed?
- Or is the pain in your thoughts? Thoughts about what happened?

Now, stop and truly be with the pain. Write your answers down below:

_____

_____

_____

_____

_____

_____

Do not pretend that everything is okay and that you are not hurt.

Insight

Pretense will only take you so far. Your invulnerability is ephemeral. It can't and won't last. One day it will let you down, at the most unexpected moment. You will be devastated, lost and petrified. Your invulnerability is a temporary camouflage created by your thoughts - your thoughts [judgments] about how/who you should be, or your judgments on how things should be.

You will realize that every time you judge, you use the verb **should**. And every time you use the verb should, you **judge**. Start replacing every "**should**" with **could**.

Stop and **truly be** with the pain.

This time, with no thoughts, therefore without judgments. Simply live the experience.

Try this exercise - Imagine yourself at a red traffic light. You are on hold. Take a moment to be with *what is* with no thoughts about *what is*. Because what is, is just is. Before the traffic light turns green, you have the opportunity to create new thoughts about what happened. You have the opportunity to keep the old ones or just keep on having no thoughts at all. Which will it be?

2. Stop and **talk** to your pain.
- Who are you? How did you get here?
- Where do you [*pain*] come from? This one is a big one. Take the time to truthfully be with it.
- What caused your sudden presence [pain]?
- What thoughts is the brain having?

Exercise
Using some of the questions above, write a letter. Write a letter to the pain. Express your anger, your hurt. You can ask as many questions as you want. In this exercise, feel free to judge your pain. With no holding back, express your feelings and allow for the emotions to come at the surface.

3. Stop and **feel**.
How are you feeling? What did you become aware of during that exercise? What are you sensing and experiencing now? Write your answers here:

_____

_____

_____

_____

_____

It is now time to write a second letter. You are, at this time, writing from the perspective of pain. You are the pain and you have lots to say. You are tired of not being listened to. You are tired of repeating yourself. Let your frustrations come out and be relieved. Please write your letter on a separate sheet and come back to step 4.

4. Stop and **listen**. Write your answers below:
     - Listen to your body. Where is the pain now?

     _____

     - Listen to your heart? How open or how tight is it?

     _____

     - As you were writing each letter, which one – your vulnerability or your invulnerability - was dictating?

     _____

     - Which one was more present, more intense?

     _____

     - What were your thoughts at the moment?

     _____

     - What can you learn from this experience?

     _____

     - What is the purpose?

     _____

As mentioned earlier, the unexpected magical source is your vulnerability. Vulnerability is at the source of all healing. From the moment you embrace your vulnerability, magic starts happening. Everything that happens, must. Everything that is, is.

Vulnerability opens the door to your authentic self. Your authentic self that is here to shine, to love, and be loved. Your authenticity allows for others to be authentic as well. We are all here with our own unique mission. Only in authenticity can it be realized.

5. Once you have embraced your vulnerability, you emerge on the other side of the mending, clearer and stronger. Stronger for all you have experienced. Stop and **accept**.

Accept the beautiful being that you are in its entirety - with its vulnerability and its invulnerability. Embrace the wound and the broken spirit with your new consciousness - The Conscious Awareness.

Conscious Awareness is
choosing to be mindful.

Insight

Mindfulness - Acceptance and being mindful in all situations gives you the clarity to see the situation for what it is. Mindfulness is contemplating each experience and situation without resistance. Mindfulness is paying attention without judgment and without reaction.

Conscious awareness is being fully present, aware and awake moment by moment. Conscious Awareness is the willingness and the decision to be aware, awake and present in each and every second. Living in conscious awareness requires you to be the action and witness of the action.

Start practicing now. Start being the *listener* of everything you say. Start being the *witness* of everything you do. The more you practice, the more you will realize that your thoughts are forcing your actions. Most of the time, you are in the '*action-reaction*' mode. From the moment you realize a thought and its upcoming negative reaction, STOP.

STOP - FEEL - LISTEN
- Is your invulnerability in the way of you seeing the *reality*?

- Are you afraid and judgmental of the people or the situation?
- Are you angry and defensive or, even offensive?

If so, you have left your *true* self. You have left your *essence*. You have moved from love into fear. It is time to embrace your vulnerability and, listen to its wisdom.

In your vulnerability rest your power.
The power of reconnection with your essence.
The power of reconnection with others – as one with you.

Let the new chiefs of the *tribe* – your authenticity and your vulnerability - help you identify your deepest gifts – your mission.

You are unstoppable. You are freedom in constant evolution!

Nkem A. DenChukwu, the author of the book titled: **"TRIBAL ECHOES: Restoring Hope"** resides in Sugar Land, Texas with her four amazing children. She was born on July 4th in the Eastern part of Nigeria, in West Africa. Nkem migrated to the United States in the fall of 1994 to further her studies. She obtained a bachelor's degree in Computer Networking, and a Master's degree in Health Services Administration. Nkem loves writing, especially to inspire others; that… is joy for her.

Contact information:
832-272-4448 (ph)
denchukwua@gmail.com
www.nkemdenchukwu.com

Chapter 18

How to Detoxify Your Life
by: Nkem DenChukwu

Ever wonder the reason(s) that you feel the way(s) you do sometimes? Have you considered why you feel tired, even after a long nap? Why you experience skin break-outs? Why you lose and gain weight? Why you have feelings of: unhappiness, joy, crankiness? Remember... "there is nothing new under the sun," you just need to find out why and how these things occur in your life.

Do not wear misery, hurt, disappointment, and all that are toxic, like a shawl. If you should wear anything, wear hope and a smile. One can only imagine, but nobody really knows how you truly feel. You know yourself better than anyone. When

> *There's no meaning to life without you. You are a priority, therefore a mission is to be accomplished.*

you make the decision to be happy regardless of the terribly bad situation you find yourself in, the resultant joy is usually priceless. Do you know that you can find that elusive peace of mind effortlessly? Of course you can. Even in the midst of a bonafide catastrophe, there is always the whiff of certain escape.

The way you choose to live your life depends on the way you think. Therefore, it is up to you to sanitize your mind, by having a positive mindset in every situation. The storms of life can weigh you down if/when you allow them to. It is a natural reaction, however unhealthy, to dwell in the miseries of the things that you have absolutely no control.

215

This chapter talks about being aware of the <u>toxins</u> in your life, and how to <u>detoxify</u> them. **Toxins** are **poisons**. They are clutters. When you clean up your closet, don't you feel relieved? Remember that when something or someone does not bring positive energy in your life, the outcome is meaningless.

Ask yourself: Am I living a healthy life: emotionally, physically, spiritually and/or socially?

How do you determine these toxins? You know the feelings of being sick. When something is not right, it must not be good. Do you know the possible toxins invading your life? These include the kinds of foods that you eat, and the negative energies around you; the not-so positive ways that you think and the negative people in your life. How do you get rid of these? Toxins cannot be ignored. You can get rid of them through a detoxification process. And, choose to be resistant to negative energies. However, when you decide to wallow in contaminants, eventually, you could lose yourself.

Have you ever...

- Looked in the mirror, and realized that the mirror image has become a stranger?
- Been in a situation, unable to breathe, yet you are breathing?
- Wondered if you will make it through the day or a situation?
- Lived in fear: Fear of the unknown and/or fear of the known?
- Laughed uncontrollably? When was the last time that you really smiled?
- Been hungry and have no hope of eating; or had food, but

216

unable to eat?

- Been disappointed for one reason or another?
- Cried because you are hurting?
- Felt that as long as you have the gift of life, you have a better shot at being a more suitable you?

Yes? It is called LIFE.

DETOXIFICATION PROCESSES
(May seem challenging, but certainly doable!)

- **STEP ONE: Eliminate bad habits.**
  When you spend time with yourself, you build a better relationship with yourself. You will be surprised at the things you will discover are your strengths and weaknesses. You will learn to appreciate yourself more.

Make a list of your bad and good habits:

BAD (TOXIC) HABITS	GOOD (NON-TOXIC) HABITS
Ex: I smoke cigarettes	Ex: I exercise three times per week.

➤ **Your mindset:** Emotional wounds are invisible wounds. They are slow death. Do not bottle up your emotions; you will explode if you do. On the same note, try not to be overly emotional. You can never go wrong on positive expressions. How you see yourself is precisely what you think and feel that you are. It may also be how others deem you to be.

"Depression" has become a household name worldwide. Science also makes it easier for many to cling to depression. Depression should NOT be in your vocabulary. From the beginning of time,  man was given the power above everything and anything negative. To be strong, you need to know your weaknesses. You should not focus on your weaknesses, rather draw your strength from them. To have hope is to have joy in your heart. "Shoulda, woulda, coulda" never count. Focus on what you can and will do, and not on what you should or could have done. Your time is now.

You are the most important part of your life. Nobody takes better care of you like you. Never give another individual the remote control of your life. You do not want to be paused, fast-forwarded or rewound, with or without your permission. Improve your thoughts. Improve yourself. Improve your life. Your daily exercise should include making a list of those needs that are good for you. Detoxify all the "shouldn't matters." Your escape should be all the "matters" that improve you.

➢ **The foods you eat**: Some people gain weight when they are happy, and some, when they are sad. Know your triggers. Starving yourself could be the reason you are gaining weight. Then ask yourself: Do I eat unnecessarily? **Bottom-line:** Having a positive mindset helps you balance

218

your diet. Eating right should be one of your good habits.

- ➤ **Your-all-season drinks:** Excessive consumption of alcohol and sugar makes you gain or lose weight, your skin breaks out, you age rapidly, and it slows down your metabolism. Health professionals say, occasional consumption (considering your health status), would not hurt. However, water is the sweetest, most natural drink on Earth. Acquire a taste for water. You can never go wrong with it.

Make a list of the drinks that you favor most:

ALCOHOLIC DRINKS	NON-ALCOHOLIC DRINKS	HOW OFTEN DO YOU DRINK?
Vodka	Water	
Red Wine	Soda	
Beer	Juice	
Palm Wine	Flavored Water	
	Milk	

- ➤ **Bowel movement:** This is an exercise that should be a daily routine, at least one or more times. Why? Because this exercise cleanses your digestive systems, and gives you the "ahhhh…" relief. When you do not have a regular bowel movement, it becomes a resident in your body, and it is a toxic leftover.

- ➤ **You and Fitness:** Do you exercise at all, too much or too little? Do you work-out to impress or look like others, or because you understand that it is a necessity to do so? **Bottom-line:** Have the proper exercise routine to fit your body type and health status.

> **STEP TWO**: **Eliminate some of the friends in your life. Make a list of who they are.**

Many people confuse what friendship is. True friends are all-season *kinda* friends. Friendship is a garden that needs constant tendering and nurturing by two or more people. However, some friends are toxic. They are like cancer of the bone. When you allow toxic friends or behaviors to be part of your life, they eventually destroy you. You need to understand the basis for your friendship, that is, the reasons that you are friends. Ask yourself, "does this friend bring positive or negative energy?" If your friendship is based on material things, then it is unhealthy, and a seasonal kind. This exercise applies to everyone: friends, couples, siblings, and even neighbors. I bet you know those that should not be in your life.

Make a list of your good friends and the not-so good ones. Treat this exercise like a business deal. It is nothing personal. Your well-being is your business, and should be handled well.

POSTIVE (FRUITFUL) FRIENDS	NEGATIVE (TOXIC) FRIENDS
Ex: Maggie (She helps me stay focused)	Ex: Carl (He always speaks negatively)

There is a difference between good and bad; it is called **choice**.

❖ **STEP THREE**: Manage Emotions Under Pressure

How do you manage emotions under pressure? It depends on you and your thoughts. When you take deep breaths, they calm your soul, and your body gets this message. Then, the body and soul become one, and are positively working together to soothe your actions. To be able to manage your emotions especially under pressure, your name should become **patient.** Being patient does not come easy. It is a "virtue." Panicking or stressing under pressure only intensifies unnecessary emotions. You should manage pressure through your emotions instead.

➢ **Living Single**

When you are living single, it could be by choice or not. Being single does not make you less than, or a greater individual than the one who is not. Some people are happier being single than being married, for a number of reasons. Knowing your strengths and weaknesses is a major factor in the way that you relate with yourself, and others. Again, to be strong, you need to know your

221

weaknesses. Never focus on your weaknesses, rather draw your strength from them. But when you embrace your weaknesses, you are living in bondage. This means that you are not living, but merely existing. This should not be the choice. Make the decision of knowing the real you. However, before you get into a relationship with another, consider the basic foundation; true friendship.

Note: One of the reasons for unhealthy and broken relationships is incompatibility. Are you compatible with yourself? People get into relationships for different reasons, and in some cases, the wrong reasons. Relationships with self, between couples, friends, siblings, neighbors or/and co-workers falter or prosper due to individual factors.

> **The Union**

Now, let's talk about the relationship called marriage. God knew what He was doing when He created Eve for Adam. Marriage is meant to be a promise of lifetime love, but it is not and hasn't been for many people. It is no secret that many marriages/couples are living in misery and chaos. Many couples live  like strangers, some like cats and dogs, while others like roommates, or total strangers.

Ever pay attention to children when they play house? They play loving (or not so loving) moms and dads, husbands and wives even teachers and students. Children genuinely show love and affection in these make believe scenes. Oh, the innocence of a child! In some cases, children recreate those experiences they are familiar with based on the real life exhibits of their parents or guardians.

If you are to breathe life into your relationship, you have to re-energize yourself by focusing on positive thoughts, actions, environments, and people. This energy is transferred in your relationship with the one you are with. Work on your bad habits rather than focusing on his/hers. Schedule date nights. Go on weekend trips, making it a tradition. Pamper yourself, then your spouse. Make it a habit to look good for you, then for your spouse, because you are the first priority. Marriage is a beautiful union of love.

When you are not emotionally in-sync with the one you are with, you have nothing to hold on to. Emotional connections come through your actions and thoughts. Physical intimacy is overrated. With time, it wears off like cheap cologne. Being emotionally intimate with your spouse makes love more unique and interesting. The emotional part of a relationship is more intimate; it makes the physical part of it more intoxicating. Mutual love or feeling is as fresh as a morning breeze; as sweet as undiluted fresh palm wine. Embrace the one you love or at least, the one you are with in body, mind and spirit. This is the grace many yearn for, yet lack.

Make a list of your strengths and weaknesses, bearing in mind that your strengths are your safeguards.

YOUR STRENGTHS	YOUR WEAKNESSES
Ex: I can identify phony personalities	Ex: I cave in to peer pressure

Now let's talk about toxic relationships in a marriage.

> ➤ **Toxic Relationship in a Marriage**

On the day you tie the knot, begins a new relationship with the one you have married. This relationship should not be taken for granted, and should start with the couple trusting each other with their lives. This is the inner sanctum, where all abiding guidelines for nourishing relationships are written. The two involved are entwined, juxtaposed as nothing else could be. Breaking this bond should not come easy. For those who finally do, their reasons are compelling, and the issues could be irreparable. That's when it has become toxic.

It becomes toxic when:

- Communication breaks down - The couple lives like strangers in their home.
- The relationship begins to suffer especially when one partner is unfaithful.
- The verbal abuse... and then, it turns physical - The start of rioting emotions, the beginning of the end.
- Loss of income - One partner loses job.
- When couples lose the last bastion of being harmonious, their relationship suffers.
- In-law blues - it is no longer used tongue-in-cheek.
- And that famous last description, irreconcilable differences.

With all marriages, there are bound to be disagreements. The important thing is to know when the trajectory of your marriage is heading south. Catch it early, and just like cancer, you could save the relationship from spinning out of control. You could save you and your partner's life from drowning by taking some simple steps; forgiving until hell freezes over. By listening more and biting down on words that are rushing you in that moment of anger, you would have designed your peace to last longer, and your partner to learn a valuable lesson on relationship 101. That is, never give voice to things you would later wish you could take back.

Many people tend to lose focus on the key issues in their lives, marriages and relationships. They fail to focus on the details of what or who really matters or makes them happy or fulfilled. Also, they blindly or intentionally neglect the roots or triggers of the chaos in their unfulfilled lives. After all is said and done, do NOT lose yourself while trying to fix what cannot be resuscitated.

> ### ➢ Married, but Single

Are you married, but single at the same time? Are you in a relationship with a possible stranger? Is this possible? Absolutely! Many couples are living separate lives under one roof, for different reasons. Some of the reasons for unhealthy and broken relationships are incompatibility, lack of humility, no love, and unhealthy childhood orientations. Some people say "I do" for all the wrong reasons. You do not always get back what you give.

Ask yourself, "Am I in an abusive relationship?" What are the early signs? Different women hold on to unhealthy relationships for a reason like: for the sake of the children. They forget that when they lose themselves, their reason for staying in the  first place is defeated. Most times, when you are being emotionally and physically abused, your vision and beliefs are overloaded. You become confused and terrified. I know that many people hide their unhappiness behind a smile, make-up, good looks, jokes, or by

225

becoming introverts to avoid being asked *why* and *how*. Behind every tear and smile is the truth in every heart.

Make a list of what you know (not assume) are the reasons that you feel single while married OR why and how you came to be in this unhealthy relationship.

Internal Contributing (Toxic) Factors	External Contributing (Toxic) Factors
Ex: I have lost intimacy with my husband	Ex: I work long hours and spend less time

In the midst of your *helter skelter* life, always remember:

- Never undermine the significance of the positive strengths within you.
- Capture your dreams by being proactive in making them happen.
- Open your eyes and heart to inspirations starting with you.
- Remember not to battle with all those things that lurk in the dark, including fears.
- Let that light in your heart be exhumed.
- Make each day your best day.
- Your freedom depends on your strength.
- Never feed on what makes you weak.
- Your attitude is one of your best accessories. Wear it well.
- Knowing the difference between what you NEED and WANT, does matter. Therefore, it is very important to prioritize your needs. Wants are perks. Work toward achieving those necessary needs, but not at the expense of

your well-being.
- When goals are reached, do not lose focus; remember that YOU are still one of your priorities.
- Life is meant to be lived well...no matter what.
- Never try to fit in. Being who you are is what makes you stand out.

This is also what I know...

I know that when you are determined and focused, the sky bears no limit. Learn to avoid unnecessary distractions. Only the dead are hopeless. You may fail in an attempt to achieve a goal, but you have the power to keep moving. When you lack self-love, you lack almost everything. Love yourself more. Each day is an opportunity that you are given to make differences in your life, and in the lives of others. It is therefore, necessary to think positively, cleanse your mind, and filter toxic people in your inner circle or around you. The way that you live or do not live your life is your choice, choose wisely.

> *There is no hopelessness in life because life is the reason for hope.*

One of the most critical decisions that you need to make is to decide what to do with the time that you have been blessed with. Time is a gracious gift. Make each moment a good story to remember. Focus on this moment, rather than dwell on the days that are past, or still ahead, or on those things that are out of your control. Be grateful for the free gift of life. The gift of life means that you are given the gift of hope, and the chance to be happier. There is so much more in life; it is called Life. So live it and love it. You are worth it!

227

QueenKay is a mother of two young boys, Chika and Lota, a multi-faceted entrepreneur, writer, enthusiast, and optimist. She moved to the United States from Nigeria when she was 18-years-old. After living in the Washington, DC area for a few years, she relocated to Los Angeles, California. Her desire to realize her creative passions led her to Hollywood. Nevertheless, she soon found herself taking a detour, to follow her heart's pathway. After falling in love and getting married, QueenKay's true-life, fairytale romance ended tragically. Ironically, the ending of her romance was the beginning of her Reconstruction and Transformation and the very catalyst of her First book, *The Reconstruction and Transformation of QueenKay*.

Contact information:

www.queenkay.com

Chapter 19
Standing in Times of Weakness
by: QueenKay

Four years ago, I found myself suddenly a widow and single mother. My husband, Charles who I planned on spending the rest of my life with passed away after a 2-year battle with bone marrow cancer. My boys were six and three respectively and I had no idea how I would pick up the pieces to make it through the day. Perhaps you have lost a loved one before, maybe even your spouse. There's no one that has the exact experience or feel the same way that you do when you experience a loss. However, you can share similarities to others and a deeper understanding of their struggles and can relate better with others. Perhaps you are divorced and have a child or children to care for. Maybe you have little or no spiritual, emotional, moral, financial or family support. What are you going to do? How are you going to get up and start that engine and keep it moving?

I will share with you how I got up. I will tell you how to make a list and show you how to create a new life chart that you can customize and make your future brighter than your past. My world came crumbling down and I had to pick up the pieces one at a time and patch up what I could, and start rebuilding my life. In my book 'The Reconstruction and Transformation of Queenkay' (see www.queenkay.com), I write about how my fairytale romance and marriage ended tragically and how I struggled to work from the inside to rebuild and transform. Although I am still a work in progress, I can tell you with confidence that this chapter in this book, The Unstoppable Woman's Guide to Emotional Well Being, is a window into the next chapter of my life. This could be the spark you need to get your life moving forward from the stagnation you may have found yourself in. I will provide you with very simple basic tools to guide you if you have found yourself in a similar position like I did in 2007, this is your wake up call.

You have to wake up because you need you. You heard me! **YOU NEED YOU**. You are alive because it's not your time to go yet. If you have children depending on you, you have to get up and take care of yourself so that you can take care of your children. They are depending on you. They need you to give them a sense of self and direction. Why should they follow you if you are going to lead them off a cliff?

This is the state of my mind shortly after my husband died and I became a widow and single mum.

- "Lord, maybe you should take me too. Of what good am I? He was my whole world."
- Slowly the fog started to clear and I realized that if I died or ran away, my kids would be in worse shape than I was. So I made a decision to live. I didn't want to live just by waking up every day and doing the mundane tasks and things we normally do to get through the day, I wanted to live a life of purpose. A huge part of me had died on the day my beloved passed away and there was no life support machine to revive me.
- I grasped unto the only being I was sure of, GOD. Even though confused and in a zombie-like state, I still believed a little spark of life was all I needed. An ignition.
- I read books to help me understand why I was still here and I listened to motivational audio CDs. I repositioned my mind on things that would build me up.

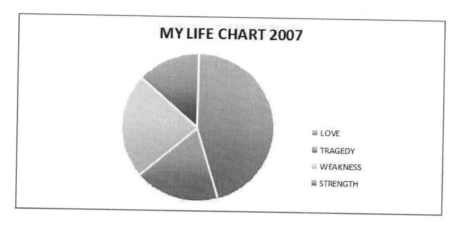

MY LIFE CHART 2007

- LOVE
- TRAGEDY
- WEAKNESS
- STRENGTH

Your will to survive has to surpass your lack of wanting to live, or live a life of real purpose. You have to find a reason to not just live, but thrive. We are all gifted with so many talents and abilities. If we do not nurture them, they become latent and die.

So, I spent the last 4 years pushing myself and rebuilding my broken spirit from the inside out. One of the things I decided to do was to write my experiences in a book. I felt my story was so uniquely different that it would resonate with so many people. I got sidetracked and lost focus so many times. I faced many obstacles including the threat of losing my home and the business I inherited from my late husband. I became a warrior. I didn't want to be homeless and not be able to provide for my kids. I started building my vision board. I knew that the life I was living was still heavily linked to that of my late husband so I had to carve out my new life from the pieces that lay bare before me. It didn't happen overnight. It's been four years since it happened and I can tell you I made strides that I would never have believed were possible. I would never have known unless I made that first step. You can too!

You have to make it! For you first and then for your children. Here are a few things you must do. Sort of like a "single mum survival kit":

- Get up and stop feeling sorry for yourself. You are not alone.
- Identify who you are and who you want to be.
- PRAY.
- Seek counseling. You need tools to help you in creating your life path.
- Write down what you want to achieve to make a better life for you and your child or children.
- Begin to execute those plans. Do not procrastinate. You will find yourself years down the line wondering why you didn't do things sooner. If time is any indicator, your kids are also growing older too, and very fast. If care is not taken, you will not have imparted the life skills you want to ensure they have to live a strong, independent and creative life. You must make sure you have a direct positive impact on your children. Otherwise, the world may have a direct negative impact on them. If you are emotionally well, your children see it and learn from that. Don't forget that children imitate what you do and not usually what you say. Be the change you want to see in them. It's going to be challenging but YOU CAN DO IT!
- Start checking off your accomplishments to encourage yourself to write new goals down. You will be amazed at how much you have done and you will be challenged to climb to greater heights.

Now that you have begun to visualize a better future for yourself and your family, doesn't that make you feel good on the inside? Good. I want you to keep in touch with me regarding your progress, because I really do care that growth is taking place and not stagnation. God has a great purpose He planted in each of us and just because you find yourself temporarily as a single mother, it doesn't mean that you will be in that position permanently.

If you do decide that you want to date or get married again, you have to make sure you are not bringing someone into your space that will bring down the solid foundation you are building. I dated a few guys after my hubby passed and I realized that it wasn't a good idea at the time. First of all, I was still grieving and not really dealing with it very well. I was a completely broken soul and craved the attention of someone who could remind me of what I had. My late hubby was an incredible human being who made an impact on my life and touched many people's lives in a very amazing way. There's almost no substitute for such a person. I had to learn that lesson the hard way. I needed to repair my broken heart by working on myself first. By trying to fill the vacuum I was not dealing with the issue.

So not only was I a single mum and widow, I was carrying a huge financial responsibility. It seemed as though it was being compounded with emotional burdens. The men I dated wanted more from me than I could give them. They wanted me to love them the way I loved my husband. They wanted time from me that I didn't have. My children are my primary responsibility and I guard them like a hawk. Until I dealt with the loss, I couldn't go forward.

"Until I completely purged myself of the pain by putting it all in my first book, I felt incomplete."

It is important to have a standard for what you want in a relationship. Otherwise, you will find yourself wasting away precious time with someone who is not deserving of you. You will find that spending time with a man just to say you have a man is taking away valuable time that could be spent building up your children to become amazing human beings and leaders of tomorrow. I love making lists or asking probing questions that help me in my decision making process.

Here's one list that helps me:

- Does the man have similar beliefs in God and family as you do? This quickly eliminates you wasting time with the wrong person. It's not that you cannot get along with someone of a different religious background, it's that what you have has to be so solid that it can stand the test of time and trials. Having a like-minded partner makes a huge difference and creates less friction when it comes to beliefs and family values. Challenges will come, how will you deal with them?

- Does he have past issues or emotional baggage that will affect what you are building if he brings it into your relationship? How will it affect your children's lives?

- Is he capable of providing for your family or contributing greatly to what you are providing for your household? Believe it or not, finances are very important and after the novelty has worn off, you are going to wake up to the reality that you both have to make sure that your finances are working well together for your family. If he has children of his own that he is bringing into the family, it is important that there is a proper merger of emotions and financials to make it work.

It is important to note that none of these points or questions matter if you haven't already started to work or have worked on yourself. You will keep attracting the wrong person if you haven't taken the time to work on you. In school you don't graduate to the next class if you don't pass the final exam. So in life, you can't move on to the next chapter if you don't learn the life lessons. It's certainly not easy to examine one's self and constructively criticize or receive criticism from others too that will enable you to grow. However, for true growth and maturity to take place, that is exactly what you have to do. You have to be open to listening and learning. How can you help your children and others to cope with these kinds of challenges when you haven't learned to cope with yours? Strive to be that woman that will be there for others like you so that we can help build emotionally strong and stable women. So years later after rebuilding myself, my life chart looks like this:

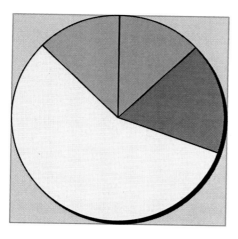

Here's the breakdown of the diagram above:
☑ CHALLENGES My Peace
☑ STRENGTH comes
☐ PEACE/LOVE/JOY/ HAPPINESS
☑ UNLIMITED POTENTIAL

from GOD. The love I feel is from within my spirit and from my family and friends. I am happy because I am living a life that has been tested and I have a better understanding of how to deal with many challenges. I am still a work in progress. I discovered strength that I didn't know I possessed and now I can tap into it and not just help myself but also others. I do not label my weaknesses as such because I choose to consider them as challenges because I am an overcomer and I will overcome them. I believe we all have potential within us to become great. However, it is up to you to stretch your vision and to push yourself to attain your highest potential. Do not limit yourself. Do not settle for less. How does your life chart look? Start building it now.

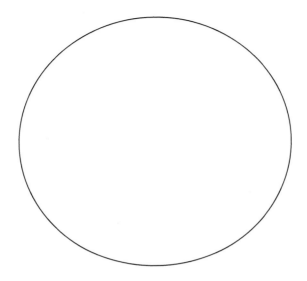

 Cynthia Fitch is a very seasoned Accounting Professional with over 16 years experience in the Accounting and Auditing industry, focusing on Financial Auditing, Internal Audit, and Compliance Auditing for several notable CPA firms including the former Big 6 Firm, Arthur Andersen. She is also a former instructor for Sawyer College (IN), where she taught Principles of Accounting and Business Math.

She is currently the President of S.C. Fitch Enterprises, Inc. which provides financial and operational consulting to small to mid-size businesses and audit assistance to CPA firms. The company also owns and operates Amateur Sports News Network, an online media magazine which covers youth athletics in the Chicagoland area. You will often find Cynthia or husband Steve, on the field or courtside covering our youth athletes in action.

Mrs. Fitch is a registered CPA in the State of Illinois and has obtained her Real Estate License. She is an active member of National Association of Black Accountants (NABA) and Illinois CPA Society. She also serves as a Commissioner on the Village of Matteson, IL Parks and Recreation Commission. Cynthia is an honors' graduate from Chicago State University with a Bachelor of Science degree in Accounting.

Contact information:
www.scfitchenterprises.com
www.amateursports365.com
cfitch@sefitch.com
708-201-1781

Chapter 20

Your Map to Financial Prosperity
by: Cynthia Fitch

Financial Management 101:
Understanding Money, Financial
Principles and Wealth Building... an
Unstoppable Must!

One thing that is essential for an Unstoppable Woman's emotional well being is to have a handle on her finances. When I say this ...I mean more than just being able to pay your bills....Do you know what you are currently worth? What is your plan for 5 years from now? Do you have funds to survive if a major tragedy or lay off occurs? What about retirement? If you die, do you have a Will in place for execution? Do you really have a financial plan or are you just taking things day by day? We all know that finances or lack thereof, is one issue that stresses the HECK out of us. You know what I mean...issues like:

- constantly dealing with the worry of how we are going to pay this bill or that loan
- whether can we borrow from Peter to pay Paul (knowing dog-gone well we don't have the money to pay either of them, so hopefully a smile and dinner works ☺)
- praying that this is not the day your water or lights will be cut off
- or thanking GOD you have caller ID so that you can avoid those constant calls from bill collectors

Sound familiar? Most of us are just trying to get through this month without breaking down, let alone planning for 5 years from now. Please know...ladies you are NOT ALONE! Money problems affect most of us no matter what our income level is and it is a *BEAST*. This stress can cause a myriad of problems including depression, reduced work productivity, high blood pressure, migraines, strains on relationships, divorce, drug use, and even suicide in severe cases, if they're not addressed.

Unfortunately, our culture associates your bank account with your worth, and we have bought into this philosophy. So before going into discussing financial matters...I need for you to know this:

YOUR WORTH IS <u>NOT</u> TIED TO YOUR WALLET!!!

You must always remember who created you, whose child you are, and that you have wonderful characteristics and talents. Your wonderful acts of love and concern when you are caring for your family, homes, and community, which are NOT financially rewarded, are priceless. Your worth is immeasurable!!!!

That being said, an Unstoppable Woman needs to know where she is financially, so that she can properly plan for her future.

For many years, even though I was an accountant/auditor, I was very disillusioned about my own financial picture. My husband and I were both working in our fields making decent money, owned our home, and we were able to pay all our bills on time, with no problem. By most folks standards, we were doing well and we thought we had a good handle on our finances. Unfortunately, this couldn't have been further from the truth. We got a rude awakening by this thing called "LIFE" (Those Unexpected Incidents that Fudges Up Everything!), to put it mildly. We went through a period where Murphy's Law kicked our butt! In a six month period, we had a death in the family (uninsured family member), a child with a broken arm, I got laid off and to top it all off, we got hit with identity theft to the tune of $5,800. We had our plan intact for when life was peachy, but not for when life throws you a curve ball. It took a few years, but I had to re-educate myself and improve our financial literacy.

In this chapter, you will be taking a journey into understanding how to do a Self-Audit of your financial picture, and the formula to getting on the path to wealth building. Now for this journey, I'm going to ask that you be as **honest** and **candid** as possible. Answer the questions as accurately as you can, and don't just pick the answer that sounds good or you think I'd want to hear if I was there with you. You can't know where you are going until you understand where you have been and where you are now.

Before writing this chapter, I wanted to get a pulse on the financial awareness of my family and friends, so I developed a simple survey asking a few basic questions on financial awareness. Take a few minutes to truthfully answer the following questions to get an idea of your overall awareness:

1. How often do you check your credit score?
2. How often do you reconcile (compare) your bank book or bank accounts to your records?
3. Do you have life insurance and a will?
4. Besides your 401K, do you have a stock portfolio?
5. Have you ever taken a basic accounting class or seminar?
6. Do you know what the basic accounting equation is?
7. Do you own your home or rent?
8. What kind of car(s) do you currently own?
9. How did you select the person that does your accounting or taxes?
10. Have you ever shopped in a Consignment Shop or Thrift Store?

It was very concerning to see that the results of my poll/questionnaire indicated that almost 30% of those polled have not checked their credit, and don't reconcile their bank accounts. According to the 2009 National Council on Economic Education, *"only 19 states require the testing of student knowledge in Economics; four fewer than in 2007. The recent economic downturn has brought nationwide attention to the dangers of an economically and financially illiterate society."* It is truly apparent that Financial Literacy should be mandatory before graduating High School, especially in this economy.

What is Money–And How Do I Use It?

So what is money?   It is any legal tender that allows you to obtain goods and services from another.

Money can't make you rich unless you understand its power and use it wisely. Money can't buy you happiness or love, but with proper usage it can buy you out of the rat race. It is important to remember, cash is only one asset and it is what it is. It makes more sense to obtain assets that can make you more cash than you paid for it.   For example, if you buy a house for $20,000 from an auction, that is worth $60,000 or you purchase stock at $25/share and by year's end it's worth $40/share. That's 'Money making Money.'

Improve your Financial Literacy - Understanding Basic Financial Terms, The Accounting Equation, and Cash Flow.

When I was studying for the CPA exam, our instructor from Beckers taught us what they called pneumonics, which are words where the letters are the first letter in other words to a phrase or term we needed to remember. Well "ALOE" is one pneumonic that I feel everyone should become acquainted with.

"ALOE"

A-L=OE

The Accounting Equation

Assets - Liabilities = Owners Equity (Worth)

It is very important to understand this equation and its components because the better you understand it, the better decisions you will make to increase your worth. So let's get an understanding of what these words mean and how they tie into your personal finances or business you may be starting.

So what is ALOE, and what does it mean for me? Well let's first get you familiar with a few key financial terms then I'll break it down for you.

Assets - Put quite simply, they are resources, things owned or prepaid expenses. Examples include cash, investments, receivables (what people owe you), inventory, prepaid insurance, land, equipment, vehicles, and furnishings.

Liabilities - Are obligations (what you owe others), and unearned revenues; examples include accounts payable (your unpaid bills), loans payable, wages payable, interest payable, customer deposits.

Owners Equity – Also known as "Net Assets" is what you or your company is worth. It is what you own, minus what you owe. It is comprised of the revenue you bring in minus the expenses you have paid out to date for the year, plus what you have saved from previous year's earnings.

To simplify things for this chapter I only listed the ones in the equation. There are more basic accounting terms you may want to familiarize yourself with. I recommend you search accounting or financial terms online on sites such as: www.accounting coach.com.

Balance Sheet – also known as a "Statement of Financial Position" - which reports assets, liabilities, equity or worth at a specific date. It provides a snapshot of what you or a company owns, owes and is worth at a point in time. For example, on December 31, 2010, XYZ Company or perhaps Mrs. X, has $150,000 in assets (owns), $100,000 in Liabilities (owes), and Owners Equity of (is worth) $50,000. The Accounting Equation for this would look like this:

$$A\ (OWN)\ -\quad L\ (OWE)\ =\ OE\ (WORTH)$$
$$\$150,000\ -\ \$100,000\ =\ \ \$50,000$$

An example of a Balance Sheet for this person or business is shown on the following page:

XYZ COMPANY Statement of Financial Position December 31, 2010		
Assets	**Liabilities and Net Assets**	
Assets:	**Liabilities:**	
Cash (on hand and in bank), Investments, Receivables (money owed to you), Prepaid Expenses, Equipment, Vehicles, Land, Buildings, and other Assets $150,000	Accounts payable (money you owe for bills), Taxes Owed, Unpaid Mortgage Balance, Other Liabilities	$100,000
	Total liabilities	**$100,000**
	Net assets (Equity):	
	Your Net Income (Total Income minus your total Expenses). Plus Saved Net Income from Prior Years.	$ 50,000
	Total Net assets (Equity)	**$50,000**
Total Assets $150,000	**Total Liabilities and Net Assets**	**$150,000**

There are a few things I want you to notice here:

1. The Accounting Equation A-L=OE is imbedded within this Report. If you look at total for each side of the report you

see that they both equal $150,000. The equation shown here is:

A=L+OE shown as Assets =$150K & Liabilities and Net Assets (Owners Equity) =$150K

This means your assets are equal to what you owe and what you are worth. This is just another form of the Accounting Equation.

2. The accounts are applicable to a business or can be related to a person's financial position. I wanted you to make the connection that whatever you do that has a financial impact is **your** business activity, whether you are self-employed or not, so please track it as such.

Your Financial Snapshot.

The information above I was very familiar with due to my studies in accounting...however, I only did a balance sheet on myself and my husband when it was time to purchase our home. I have to honestly admit that while I kept us on track with paying our bills, I did not continue to monitor our balance sheet and make  moves to increase our worth. That costly mistake resulted in our not being prepared for life's setbacks. So if there is anything I absolutely want you to take away from this chapter, it is for you to do the following exercise and prepare your own financial snapshot immediately. So let's get started!

To do this properly, you will need to have all of your bills, bank statements, asset appraisal reports, mortgage statements, and income receipts in front of you. If you are reading this chapter in the beginning of a month then use the last day of the previous month as your snapshot date i.e. December 31, 2011.

Step 1. Compile a list of all assets including cash, investments, receivables, prepaid expenses, etc. and obtain the estimated value of each, via statements, appraisals, etc.

Step 2. Make a list of all of your income by any source. (Pay Check, Business Income, Gambling winnings, etc.)

Step 3. Create a list of all of your bills, the due date, frequency, how much you owe, and note important information relating to each one. This can very easily be done on Excel. Here is an example of what I am asking of you:

Bills Due List

Due Date	Description	Check #	Min. Due	Balance	Phone #	Acct #
Monthly Bills						
1	Cap One	4379	$ 30.00	$59.00	800-951-6951	#XXX
1	Son (after-care)	4380	$ 265.00			
3	Health Club	AUTO	$ 10.50		866-402-2559	#XXX
4	GE Money Bank		$ 25.00	$441.00	866-396-8254	#XXX
5	T-Mobile	4381	$ 75.00		800-243-4350	#XXX
7	Brinks	AUTO	$ 29.95		(800) 445-0872	
9	Public Storage		$ 66.00		708-895-8856	#XX, Space# XX
9	ValueCity		$ 35.00	$ 1500.00	800-428-8818	#XXXX
10	Chase (Mortgage)	4382	$ 962.95		800-548-7912	#XXXX
14	NICOR	4383	$ 150.00		(888) 642-6748	3x-x0-x0-0000

						3
26	Comcast		$105.00		888-262-6300	#XXXX
26	Vonage	AUTO	$60.57		866-243-4357	#XXXX
28	Sallie Mae		$70.00	$565.00	888-272-5543	#XXXX
30	BrightStart (Oppenheimer)	AUTO	$50.00		877-432-7444	#XXXX
Totals			**$1,934.97**	**$2,565.00**		

Periodic Bills						
Semi-Annual	State Farm - Auto	4384	$253.80		773-933-0066	#XXXX
ANNUAL	Sam's Club			$43.50		#XXXX
ANNUAL	State Farm (Home)			$670.00	773-483-0000	Policy# XXXX
ANNUAL	City of Chicago		$-	$60.00		
QTRLY	City of Chicago		$-	$130.00		#XXXX
Totals			**$253.80**	**$903.50**		

Total Monthly Bills		**$1,934.97**
Total Paid		**$1,448.40**
Monthly Bill to be Paid		**$486.57**
Total Debt		**$2,565.00**
Total Paid		**$779.37**
Total Debt Balance		**$1,785.63**
Total Periodic Bills		**$1,157.30**
Total Paid		**$253.80**
Amount Due		**$903.50**

It's also a good idea to add a column for the company's website, a column for notes, and indicate whether you've paid the bill. Make sure you enter as much pertinent information as possible. You can even add special notes, such as the contact person you last spoke to while disputing a charge or working out a payment arrangement with a creditor that keeps bugging you with those nagging phone calls. ☺

Using a schedule such as this one will help you keep track of all of your outstanding accounts, expenses and debt in one place. This allows you to get a full picture to make better decisions regarding timing of payments on outstanding bills/debt, strategies for eliminating certain debt, if you have enough to pay more than the minimum on a credit bill this month, etc. Also, knowing the date your bills are due and which ones are automatically taken out of your account can help you plan your cash flow to ensure the funds are in your account to cover automated withdrawals. Keeping a handle on this can prevent overdrawing your account and accumulating those dreadful NSF fees.

Step 4. Enter your bills on a calendar by its due date along with the days you get paid from your job or business. This will help you with a visual picture of when stuff is due and what you can pay based on when your funds come in to better manage your cash flow. See the following page:

XYZ CALENDAR

SUN	MON	TUES	WED	THUR	FRI	SAT	Weekly Totals
				1 After Care $xxx CapOne (P) $xx	2 Pay Day $xx	3 Bally's $xx	Income: $x,xxx.xx Expenses: $x,xxx.xx
4	5 T-Mobile $xx	6	7 NTB $xx	8	9 Storage $xx Value City $$xx	10 Mortgage $xxx	Income: $x,xxx.xx Expenses: $x,xxx.xx
11	12	13	14 NICOR $xx	15 State Farm $xxx	16 Pay Day$x,xxx	17	Income: $x,xxx Expenses: $x,xxx
18	19	20	21	22	23 ComED $xxx	24	Income: $x,xxx Expenses: $x,xxx
25	26 Metra $xxx	27	28 AT&T $xxx	29 Sallie Mae $xxx	30 Bright Start $xx		Income: $x,xxx.xx Expenses: $x,xxx.xx

Total Income for the Month	**$xxx.xx**
Total Expenses for the Month	**$xxx.xx**
Net Income for the Month	**$xxx.xx**

Step 5. Total your monthly expenses, your periodic bills, and credit card or loan balances.

Step 6. Identify expenses that are to be paid within one year and then those that are to be paid over several years, like mortgages and other loans. For those expenses that occur **monthly**, estimate those costs for 12 months to get an estimated annual total. Note the total of all your **unpaid** expenses due within 1 year; those are your Current Liabilities. The total of all your **unpaid** expenses due over 1 or more years, are your Long-Term Liabilities.

Step 7. Total your monthly income from all sources.

Step 8. Enter the totals of your assets items and liabilities on your balance sheet and add them up to determine Total Assets.

Step 9. Calculate your Net Assets (Equity or worth) by subtracting your liabilities from your assets.

Step 10. Subtract your Expenses from your total Income to determine your Net Income and add this amount to your Net Assets.

Now you know where you are financially at this moment. You have literally taken a financial snapshot. This process may take some time to accomplish, especially if you do it long hand or manually in a spreadsheet. But knowing how to do it the long way will help you to understand each component and how things are being added up to determine your snapshot. Good news! There are many automated software packages that are awesome to help you determine your financial picture, plan for your future and monitor your progress such as Quicken, Ace Money, YNAB and Money Express. Financial software can help you get a better picture of where your money is going.

Now that you know where you are you can determine where you are going and you can do the following:
- **Set your short term and long term goals, (bill pay off, vacations, retirement, etc.).**
- **Make a budget and stick to it.**

- **Include your short term and long term goals in your budget.**
- **Include setting aside funds for emergencies.**
- **Include fun stuff in your budget; it will keep you from falling off the wagon.**

Once you have created a workable budget, please try your best to stick to it. Ask a friend, family member or your financial advisor to help you with staying on task.

Planning for Tax Time

Tax time brings about mixed emotions for many people. For some, it is a piece of cake, for others it can be a pain in the neck. I know it has been both for me, at one time or another. Here are a few pointers for how you can save money on tax preparation costs and prepare to spend your refund wisely when you finally get it back from Uncle Sam.

- **Shop around.** Whether you choose to patronize a franchise or a small company, inquire about special programs or discounts that may be available. There are also numerous private preparers, easy to use software, and on-line services that provide similar quality service. So be sure to do your homework and ask for referrals.
- **Be organized and thorough.** Keep all receipts for expenses greater than $25. There are many sophisticated systems for paperwork organization on the market. However, if you don't have the funds for these systems, obtain 12 large envelopes, label one for each month and put all of your receipts in them each month religiously. For all other tax related paperwork, get an expanding file folder and label each section with the major categories of paperwork needed to prepare your return.

- **E-File on line.** If you have a simple return i.e. 1040EZ or 1040 with no itemized deductions, it is not necessary to pay upwards of $125 for someone to prepare your taxes. If you can access a computer with internet capability, you can E-File with the IRS right on-line.

Now for that timeless question…"What do I do with all this refund money?"

Well, if you are like me…our first instinct is to go shopping. From my inquisitions, the most popular things purchased with tax refunds are cars, jewelry or clothes (including furs). I must admit I am guilty of this as well, purchasing countless number of purses, boots, watches, rings, and trips with my tax refund. After dealing with the stress of tax time…. there's nothing better than comfort power shopping. Can I get a witness!! However, after many years of blowing my tax refund, I realized that none of these things placed me closer to my financial goals. If a car, jewelry or clothes are not a must have, why not invest your money towards an appreciating asset or something that will benefit you or others instead? Here are a few great options:

- ❖ **Knock out those Bills**: Use your return or at least half of it to pay down one or more of your bills, preferably the credit card account(s) with the highest interest rate(s).
- ❖ **Purchase Invaluable Assets**: An appreciating asset increases in value over time. Examples such as an IRA, or individual Stocks or Bonds, Real Estate, Tax Certificates, etc. are a few of many great choices.
- ❖ **Bless someone else**: Make a contribution to your favorite charitable organization. Contributions to legitimate charitable organizations are tax deductible. Be sure to obtain a receipt and keep it in your tax files.
- ❖ **Start your own business**: The gratification of fulfilling your dream of being your own boss with possibly employing and empowering others is immeasurable. In addition, there are

numerous tax benefits to having a home-based business.

Secrets of the Wealthy

Please notice I said WEALTHY and not the RICH. Rich people have money for a period of time, obtain a lot of trophies, toys, clothes and rack up a lot of debt to go along with it, and sooner or later, if they don't plan properly, can and will end up broke. Wealthy people take their money and invest in profitable assets including property, businesses, stocks, bonds, rights, patents, etc. to accumulate enough money for themselves to live off of (often lavishly), and to secure financial freedom for their current family, as well as for generations to come. That's how you build a legacy.

> ➤ **Vehicle Purchases** - Are you one of those people who buy a new car every few years? If so, please stop trying to keep up with the Jones. It's not having a new shiny vehicle every few years that makes you cool or smart, it's having a well kept vehicle that is paid for and you're getting as many years out of it without paying a note that is cool. Many wealthy people have regular cars that they drive for their everyday activities. They often have their luxury car that they use for special outings or on weekends, however this car is paid for by earnings from their assets, and are not paying a note when they are living check to check. **The lesson here is:** In this declining economy, make sure you have a clean reliable car to get you where you need to go and ride that puppy till the wheels fall off. **Use the money you save to purchase profitable assets.**

> ➤ **Consignment Wonders** - Did you know that many wealthy people, including many of your favorite stars, occasionally shop in consignment shops? Yes, I said **consignment shops, second hand stores, thrift stores;** whatever you want call it. Even the rich have realized you can often find

many **GEMS** in resale shops. I really recommend this option. Think of this way: **Is it better to have 5 fashionable suits that cost you $1,200-$1,500, or those suits for $100-$300 and use the savings to pay off your bills, and purchase profitable assets? You do the math!**

➢ **<u>Start a Business</u>** - If you have a special talent like auto repair or hair styling, instead of doing it as a hobby and getting a few free lunches or pocket change, turn your interest into a valid **BUSINESS. Have you noticed that most celebrities that have maintained their wealth, have started some type of business with their fame?** Having a business allows you to be able to write off many expenses that you can't write of personally like: office supplies, equipment, utilities, telephone, business lunches (only 50%), mileage, etc. Be sure to see your financial advisor for more details and guidance on proper tracking and reporting.

Spiritual Financial Principles

Last, but definitely not least, I want to leave you with some spiritual quotes and/or scriptures about money and financial prosperity as the Unstoppable Woman is definitely a spiritual being.

- **"And my God shall supply all your needs according to His riches in glory in Christ Jesus" (Philippians 4:19).**
- **"And God is able to make all grace abound to you, that always having all sufficiency in everything, you may have abundance for every good deed" (2 Corinthians 9:8).**

- **Empty pockets never held anyone back. Only empty heads and empty hearts can do that. ~Norman Vincent Peale**

- **When prosperity comes, do not use all of it. ~Confucius**

Scripture clearly teaches that God wants to bless His people with financial prosperity. That doesn't mean we'll all drive a Mercedes or take a Caribbean cruise every year. But if we live and give according to spiritual principles, our needs will be met and we will be blessed to help others.

That's true financial prosperity and a major sign of the "Unstoppable Woman!"

 Ina R. Threatt was born in East Chicago, Indiana on April 3, 1960.

Ina has a Ph.D. in Holistic Nutrition from Clayton College of Natural Health in Birmingham, AL. She has a Master Herbalist Degree from The School of Natural Healing in Springville, UT. Ina is a 1st Degree Black Belt as well as an Associate of Arts Degree in Fashion Design from the Fashion Institute of Design and Merchandising in Los Angeles, CA.

You can purchase her one of a kind, ladies coats and jackets at her web site. To schedule an appointment in the greater Atlanta area for individual or group Nutritional Education please feel free to contact Ina.

Contact information:
drinathreatt@hotmail.com
www.koatsnjakets.webs.com
706-383 8708

Chapter 21

Ending Self Inflicted Pain & Stress
by: Ina Threatt

When changing deeply imbedded habits, it is wise to learn to be patient with yourself. You have to constantly remind yourself that whatever you are trying to change did not happen overnight. Developing this habit is a process. It requires time to decide that you no longer want it in your life and that you are ready to eliminate or alter this habit. No matter what it is, overeating, not making time for you, listening to others' negative view of you, not being organized, etcetera. You have to realize that this is a habit and that you will slip back into it from time to time. This is okay as long as you keep working towards your goal.

The first step is to admit that you have a problem. The second step is to decide what you want to do about this problem. Finally you have to make a realistic plan on how to alter or eliminate this problem. It would be a good idea to taper off rather than trying to just quit, unless you are strong enough to do so. Once you have identified the behavior that you want to change and set realistic goals, the next step is to develop tactics that will encourage new habits and ways to stay motivated. This may even include excluding people, places and things, that are not in your best interest. It is up to you to do everything in your power to make these changes happen. You have to focus on the desired results. Telling yourself to eat right or exercise more doesn't work. If you want to make those lifelong habits go away, whatever they are, you have to do the work. Changing habits, even when the steps are small, requires a commitment. Focusing on small changes that can be maintained to stay on track is crucial. Before you take the plunge, you must be sure that you are ready and willing to do whatever it takes to feel and look your best.   Only you can take charge of your life, and the desired result will vary, based on your actions.

Mind Set and Attitude

When speaking about this vast universe, everything works on a yin and yang dynamic.   Try thinking that your attitude works exactly the same way.   When you are balanced all seems right with  the world.   You have a happy positive attitude, you are happy and temporarily content.   On the other side of positive is negative; when you are out of balance your negative attitude takes over. You become angry, and subconsciously destructive.   Depending on which mind set you happen to be in, your cells automatically conform to that particular attitude.

Control whatever you do by focusing on what you want and positive ways of achieving it.   However, negative events are a part of life and have to be dealt with in an eliminating manner. Whenever you are faced with something negative or unbalancing, the yang side up approach can be beneficial.   Yang is positive, outgoing, active and hot.   The practice of yang side up is helpful in all negative situations.   Yin on the other hand is negative, introverted, passive and cold.   Do remember however, that when you go too far in one direction, you become the contradiction of the other.   Your attitude and what goes on in your mind is your responsibility and no one else's.   Make every attempt to surround yourself with positive people, places and things as much as possible.   There are a number of groups you can join and organizations that offer support when asked properly.   By properly, I mean there may be a specific form or person involved.   Do your research.   Again look at books on this very subject, check your local bookstore. You can also go online to find a number of books, try BarnesandNobles.com or Amazon.com. Books that I have found to be helpful are "*As A Man Thinketh*" by James Allen and Napoleon Hill's "*Keys to Positive Thinking*" and of course "*The Secrets to Being an Unstoppable Woman*" by Erika Gilchrist. You can also play little games with yourself, like have positive days, or weeks to change your mood when you find yourself slipping to far into the yin. During these times, whenever something unpleasant happens, try singing or saying something upbeat to bring about a more positive feeling. It may feel strange or downright stupid at first, but remember, this is a process. Music is a great way to change your mood instantly. You can start a collection of quotes to always have and look back on. You can turn some of those sayings into chants that you repeat throughout the day. It is up to you to choose ways to help maintain balance and peace. List some of your favorite quotations or sayings here:

_____

_____

Spirit

Your spirit is basically how you feel overall. It's your day to day outlook at life and how you deal with each circumstance that is presented to you. From a yin/yang point of view, if you fill your spirit with more yin type thinking, you might find your  energy level too low. On the flip side, more yang type thinking would make you more anxious. Either way you will not feel your best and if you are not aware of your spiritual SELF, you can find yourself in the doctor's office due to fatigue or anxiety. In addition to staying open spiritually, hopeless and defeated thinking must be dealt with and cleared out, so as not to develop physical imbalances. Often times, individuals are not aware of their feelings being connected to their physical selves. Whenever something happens to you that causes fear, your body's natural responses include a rapid heartbeat and quicker breathing. If you can remain aware of what is happening to you physically, you have more control over what you can do at that particular moment to bring yourself back to a calmer more peaceful place. When you get into an argument, your face can reveal the level of anger you are experiencing. These are two examples that can temporarily throw you off balance if you are not careful. Your goal is to go through it and remain balanced so as not to leave any negative residue. Try really hard to keep your spirit as clean as possible to avoid picking up any unattractive energy. Physical exercise including yoga, chanting and meditation can be used to encourage you to remain motivated and focused. Deep breathing and awareness to your breath can bring about balance instantly. Calming you down and helping you think clearly. Here are five quick ways to start the calming process:

1. **Walk away**: Starting physically moving away from the situation
2. **Breathe deeply**: Give the body plenty of oxygen. This also eliminates toxins
3. **Listen to soothing music**: Allow it to alter your mood so you can think more clearly
4. **Find a tranquil place**: Go to a place that gives a sense of peace
5. **Close your eyes**: You may start to meditate, or even pray. Center yourself.

Goal Options

Having a passion in life and working towards it is the best way to keep any negative situation from taking hold of you for too long. I remember when I wanted to learn martial arts. Because it was more challenging than I had anticipated, more training was required than the suggested twice a week. In order for me to get the basics down with the proper form, I chose to take private lessons along with my regular classes. As a result of this schedule I turned down invitations that I would normally have preferred to accept. Because I had a goal to achieve and a time frame for achieving it, I chose to put things on hold or eliminated them altogether. This new attitude could create problems for those who don't really have your best interest in mind. Now is the time to become aware of your inner circle of associates. Who is really on your side?

When setting goals it is important to realize that something might have to be given up in order to achieve something else.

If your problem is food or a certain kind of food, you might try experimenting with substitutes, that way you won't feel deprived. You must allow yourself some time to get accustomed to this substitute and not give up because the taste is different. For example if your problem is chocolate, you might try carob (a tropical pod that contains a sweet, edible pulp and inedible seeds). If you are really into fried foods, you might try cooking in the oven to achieve the same crispy texture, without the oil.

If you are in a relationship and want to encourage new responses from your mate, mother or friend, you initiate a new response. Instead of silently accepting a put-down or negative comment about your weight, maybe admit this could be a factor in your life and now is the time to change it. On the other hand if you don't agree, defend yourself. Express how you feel about this comment or situation and request that a new approach be taken. Acknowledging that you have a situation that requires changing and speaking up for yourself will strengthen you every single time. You are saying, "I am aware of this and you're right, or I am aware and I don't agree." This keeps you honest with yourself and the situation has less power over you.

If you remember to keep your steps to achieving your goals small enough, you don't get overwhelmed. Then you can gradually increase the risk as you overcome each hurdle. Only you can decide what is more important and what you are willing to do to obtain that goal.

Another key ingredient towards achieving goals is to have a plan or an idea of how you are going to accomplish something. To get ideas, I think this would be the time when you are reading some type of motivational material, watching videos, listening to CDs or even attending some type of seminar. For example, if your goal is to become a paid professional speaker, you may want to attend a meeting with a speaker's association.

Keeping a written record of your habits is one way to identify which behaviors are contributing to your problem. This way you can make changes as swiftly and as often as necessary. This allows for more control day to day as opposed to trying to correct or control years of accumulation. These are lifelong steps that have to be incorporated into your daily activity.

Focus on and visualize whatever it is you want to achieve and let nothing and no one interfere with that desired result. This does not mean abandon all responsibility, however, it does mean getting creative and reprioritizing. Visualize yourself having whatever your goal is and conduct yourself in a manner as though you have already reached it and show gratitude. Concentrate on your goals and find ways to make them happen. Use all of your resources: the internet, book stores and talking to other people. Don't be afraid to ask for help whenever necessary. Experiment with some of your own ideas, which I encourage and feel is the best of all. So as not to alienate anyone and not to create any ill will, try to barter for favors and make trades for things you want, but can't pay for. This makes for a win/win situation and might make others more of an ally. Find someone you look up to and/or someone who has succeeded in this area and ask for help.

The road to success is rarely a straight line and keeping motivated can sometimes be easier said than done. There are times when you just don't feel like exercising or you want a piece of chocolate cake, maybe two, and it is perfectly acceptable as long as you realize you cannot give in every time you feel like it. This is what moderation is all about, not depriving yourself of little things that make you happy and at the same time not letting them get out of control. This gives you a sense of accomplishment and strengthens your confidence.

Do not under any circumstance berate yourself if you find that you need to take time off from whatever you are working on. This can be motivating and bring you back refreshed and ready to continue with new enthusiasm. If you find that you want more and more time off, this might be a good time to take a close look at what is going on and do something about it before you lose interest and give up all together. One way to instill discipline is to set deadlines and meet them. Schedule daily, weekly and monthly tasks and check them off as they get completed. If the people around you are not supporting you in your personal growth, you may have to re-prioritize these relationships. Your emotions cannot be a factor here as painful as this might be. You are what is important. I suggest that you find ways to motivate yourself and not look too much outside.

For example, when exercising, if you have a camcorder, set it up in front of you while you do your workout and then watch yourself to track your progress. You will be able to see day to day results and see yourself gradually changing. Do something fun like change outfits everyday or get really creative to help you through your workouts.

Success

Do you know what the phrase "The Grass is Greener on the Other Side" means? Basically all it means is that you think something is one way only to find out that it is not. Have you ever wanted something and worked so hard for it and then have the harsh reality hit you, making you realize that this is not what you really wanted after all? Could that be maybe because too much energy is put into a lot of things that have no long term meaning leaving an emptiness and a desire for still something else?

When it comes to success, I think flexibility and adversity go hand in hand. In a similar way, failure and the stamina to persevere are the yin and yang of one another. I have learned the hard way, that just because you prepare and plan for what you want to happen, there is always another element that might somehow prevent your efforts from being realized, for that purpose. Flexibility on your part allows you to learn something that may not have originally been your focus, and at the same time help you to remain balanced and motivated while working towards your original goal. Setbacks and adversity make for changes that perhaps you had not anticipated. Being flexible allows you to see that there is always more than one way to do something. Whatever the obstacle is that is in your way can be viewed as a challenge and stimulate your mind to reach beyond your comfort zone.

Unstoppable ladies are prepared to endure the long run, and they understand that there are bumps along the way. The first step is to discontinue the self abuse.

Dr. Kimberly Middleton received her medical degree at the University of Illinois College of Medicine, Chicago in 1997. She completed her residency in Family Medicine at the University of Illinois and was fellowship trained in Maternal and Child Health at West Suburban Hospital in Oak Park, Illinois. She managed high risk pregnancies and deliveries and provided follow-up care for newborns and children who were at risk for poor outcomes. She is board certified in Family Medicine and focuses on women's and children's health; including family healthcare, preventative health maintenance, bio-identical hormone replacement for women, nutrition, anti-aging and management of Autism and ADHD.

Dr. Middleton is a member of the American Medical Association and an active fellow of the American Academy of Anti-aging and Regenerative Medicine. She lectures regularly throughout the Chicagoland area on topics related to wellness, nutrition, supplements, nutrient depletion, disease prevention and medical therapies for the treatment of menopause, autism and ADHD. She is currently in private practice in Joliet, Illinois.

She was born in Chicago, Illinois, grew up in Dublin, California, and is a University of California, Berkeley Alumnus. In her free time she enjoys running marathons and triathlons as well as spending quality time with her husband and children.

Contact information:
1736 Essington Road
Joliet, IL 60435
312-399-7185
kmiddletonmd@midservices.com

Chapter 22

Are You Depleting Your Wellness?
by: Kimberly Middleton, M.D.

Maalox, Lipitor, Metformin, birth control pills—do you have any of these in your medicine cabinet? Well, if you do, you are likely losing important nutrients that your body needs, resulting in unintended, long-term health consequences. In fact, one of the most overlooked side effects of prescription drugs is nutrient depletion.

According to the IMS Institute for Healthcare Informatics, in 2010 over $307 billion dollars was spent on prescription drugs in the United States, a 2.3% rise from the previous year[1]. In fact, in 2007-2008 nine out of ten American adults were reported to be taking at least one prescription medication. The fact is that our country has been labeled the most overprescribed country in the world. We have become a "pill popping" society, relying on prescription drugs as a quick fix for all of our physical, emotional and sexual problems. Many people reach for these pills before ever attempting healthier choices such as diet and exercise to prevent and treat common lifestyle-related conditions.

Despite numerous studies that document that prescription and over-the-counter medications deplete essential nutrients in the body, the companies that manufacture these drugs are not required to provide warning labels regarding this, nor are they interested in publicizing this potentially ominous data. You may be surprised to know that approximately 100,000 people die each year in the U.S. of medication that was taken as prescribed. This averages to be

[1] IMS Institute for Healthcare Informatics. www.imshealth.com

about 270 deaths per day[2]. Despite this, many prescription drugs are advertised as the only solution for most of today's health problems and very little information regarding issues such as drug-induced nutrient depletion is ever conveyed to health care professionals and most importantly, to patients like you. I've listed some of the most common prescription drugs dispensed to patients in 2010. If you are taking any of these medications or any others, it is imperative that you understand how they can influence your nutritional status. This knowledge will help to ensure that you do not fall into the trap of becoming nutrient depleted.

Let me be clear: this is *not* a plea for you to discontinue any of your medication. Nor am I encouraging you to replace any of your prescription medication with supplements or add supplements without medical advice. I strongly believe that when prescription medications are used properly, they can help individuals live healthier and longer lives. As a physician, I must advise you to consult with your primary care provider or other healthcare professional before making any changes to your current regiment.

This chapter serves as an educational tool to help provide possible explanations as to why you may be feeling some of the symptoms that you do. I also hope to reveal some possible and often, subtle side effects caused by medication. The goal here is to educate and empower you in the management of your prescription medication so that you can become a healthier you. After all, one of your greatest testimonies as an unstoppable woman is maintaining optimal health.

"Do you not know that your body is a temple of the Holy Spirit, who is in you, whom you have received from God? You are not your own; you

---

[2] *Journal of the American Medical Association* (JAMA), April 15, 1998

were bought at a price. Therefore honor God with your body," (1 Cor. 6:19-20).

Here's how the problems begin:

Nutrients are chemicals that help your body live, grow, develop, and thrive. They are required to carry out the normal functions of your body. They help the body build new tissue and repair damaged tissue, protect the body from toxic damage, boost the immune system, promote growth and provide an energy source to regulate daily body functions. Every day billions of cells in your body die and replace themselves. This involves bone remodeling, skin cell repair, and red blood cell destruction and production. Nutrients are needed to carry out these as well as other important bodily functions. When there is a lack or shortage of even one nutrient, normal physiologic mechanisms are unsupported. A by-product of medication-induced nutrient depletion is a body that potentially becomes weakened instead of healed. Since drug-induced nutrient depletion is usually a slow process, the signs and symptoms tend to be more subtle, as opposed to that of an allergic reaction to a medication, which typically occurs soon after exposure. A chronic imbalance or complete lack of critical nutrients usually begins to take a toll on your body over a course of months or years. This, however, can ultimately lead to serious health consequences. A drug's impact on nutrition also correlates with its dose, with higher doses causing more injury. If these problems are compounded by an unhealthy diet, advancing age, pregnancy, stress, multiple medications, or other medical conditions, nutrient depletion can become life threatening.

Nutrient depletion can occur in a number of ways:

1. Appetite (Nutrients are not taken in):
Some prescription medications affect your appetite. Stimulants such as Adderall and Ritalin, used to treat

attention deficit hyperactive disorder (ADHD) can reduce appetite (the class of drugs were initially advertised as diet pills) and subsequently decrease the intake of beneficial nutrients. Other drugs such as steroids can increase the desire for unhealthy foods that are high in empty calories, causing weight gain but poor nutrition.

2. **Production: (nutrients are not produced):** Some vitamins and nutrients such as vitamin K are produced by healthy intestinal flora (bacteria). With long-term or recurrent use of antibiotics, damage to healthy intestinal bacteria may lead to vitamin K deficiency.

3. **Absorption (nutrients cannot get into the body):** The stomach and intestines are lined with proteins and enzymes necessary for proper digestion and transport of essential nutrients into the bloodstream. Medications that change the lining of the gastrointestinal (GI) tract affect the absorption of these nutrients. When this occurs, even if you eat foods that are rich in vitamins and minerals, these nutrients may never reach key organs where they can be utilized. Antibiotics, while killing bacteria that cause illness, can also destroy normal, healthy bacteria that are required for nutrient absorption. Since one of the primary functions of healthy bacteria is to aid in food digestion, the result of chronic or recurrent use of antibiotics result in unpleasant symptoms such as bloating, constipation, diarrhea, abdominal pain, and belching.

Often, drugs can bind to essential nutrients and form complexes that are unable to pass through the gastrointestinal tract (GI) and into the blood stream; thus they get excreted outside of the body before ever being absorbed and utilized. The antibiotic Tetracycline has this effect, by binding to minerals such as magnesium, iron, zinc and calcium.

Antacids (Maalox, Mylanta, etc.) and proton pump inhibitors (Prevacid, Prilosec, etc.) lower the acid content of the stomach. Since high acid levels are essential for proper absorption of certain vitamins and nutrients, low levels can cause depletion of these important substances. A classic example of this is calcium which requires an acidic environment for proper absorption through the stomach and into the blood stream. When antacids and calcium are taken concurrently, the use of antacids can lead to calcium deficiency and subsequent loss in bone mineral density, resulting in an increased risk for fractures. This is especially problematic for the elderly who already have low acid levels in their stomach.

4. **Metabolism and utilization (nutrients are not available when needed):** Metabolism involves converting food into the energy and products needed to sustain life. Medications can interfere with the body's ability to metabolize certain nutrients and result in their inability to perform their intended function. For example, many studies indicate that vitamin B_6 and folate metabolism are altered in women who take birth control pills. This can lead to depression, birth defects, abnormal cervical cell growth, and other adverse conditions. Other drugs such as anticonvulsants, used to treat individuals with seizure disorders, can increase the rate in which the body breaks down vitamin D. Since the main role of vitamin D is to help the body to absorb calcium and deposit it into bones and teeth, a deficiency has the opposite effect and weakens them.

5. **Excretion (nutrients are wasted):**

Some drugs can directly increase the rate at which nutrients are excreted outside of the body. Diuretics or "water pills", used to treat high blood pressure, heart failure, and swelling, are the greatest offenders. When diuretics flush excess fluid outside of the body, they subsequently drain vitamins and minerals. If Furosemide (Lasix), is one of the medications that you take, doctors will typically prescribe potassium as well because diuretics are commonly known to increase urinary excretion of potassium. Since potassium is very important for the heart and other muscles to function properly, individuals with severe potassium deficiency might find themselves experiencing muscle cramps, nausea, vomiting, fatigue, irregular heartbeats, constipation and other symptoms that could result in hospitalization and death.

Several years ago, a 35-year-old school bus driver and mother of three, walked into my office complaining of chronic abdominal pain, bloating and episodes of constipation and diarrhea. Her symptoms were affecting her ability to work and she was desperate for relief. She had previously had a colonoscopy, biopsy, and a CAT scan of her abdomen but was told that everything was normal. She felt frustrated after complying with all of the dietary recommendations for her condition (Irritable Bowel Syndrome) but never experienced any relief.

Her past medical history included chronic fatigue and depression, which had not improved with a variety of anti-depressant medications. Sadly, she had learned to live with her symptoms since she was told it was part of the aging process. She also had a history of Type II Diabetes which was well controlled on Glucophage (Metformin). She had been taking birth control pills for over ten years and had experienced no known side effects from

271

them. With further questioning, she conveyed a longstanding history of childhood ear infections and bouts of strep throat, requiring numerous courses of antibiotics.

She was an overweight female with brittle nails and coarse, dry hair and skin. Lab investigation revealed a deficiency in almost all of her B vitamins as well as zinc. Stool testing showed abnormally high yeast levels and harmful bacteria in her intestines. This was not surprising since she had taken so many antibiotics in the past and had probably wiped out all of the beneficial organisms in her GI tract. Additionally, I discovered that she had positive allergies to strawberries and cocoa, which were foods that she craved and ate often.

I started by removing the offenders. First, her birth control pills, since these are directly linked to vitamin B deficiencies and was likely one of the sources of her fatigue and "psychological" symptoms. I also recommended that she eliminate her food allergens. Although she had not been experiencing typical allergy related symptoms, food allergies may also present as diarrhea, abdominal pain and constipation. Her food allergens might have also had an effect on her brain, contributing to her depressive symptoms.

After obtaining all results and collaborating with my patient, I established a plan. Over the next several weeks to months, she took digestive enzyme supplements to help her body break down her meals more efficiently. Probiotics (healthy bacteria) were later added to re-populate beneficial bacteria into her intestinal tract. To restore her nutrient deficiency and put her system into better balance, I added a multivitamin, a vitamin B-complex, additional calcium, vitamin D_3, fish oil and zinc. I also added sublingual vitamin B_{12} to her regiment since blood levels of this vitamin are found to be low in up to 30% of people who take Metformin

chronically.[3] My patient went the extra mile and purchased
Boswellia and Olive Leaf extract after reading how both aid in
intestinal repair. Her plan included increased water and fiber
intake combined with medicinal foods such as okra, cabbage, and
flax seeds.

The treatment plan that was established showed excellent results.
Within several months, her mineral levels were restored and she
reported a huge improvement in her energy level and mood. Her
abdominal symptoms resolved and her dry nails and hair became
healthy again. To her surprise, she had also lost weight and was
back to normal balanced health.

Unfortunately, the above scenario is very common. Symptoms are
treated but drug-induced nutrient depletion is ignored. As a result,
patients walk around for years feeling unhealthy, yet they are left
without an explanation for their symptoms.

Table 1. Symptoms of Nutrient Deficiency

Nutrient	Symptoms of Deficiency
Calcium	blood pressure irregularities, fractures, muscle spasms, osteoporosis (bone loss), tooth decay
Glutathione	poor balance, poor coordination, poor immune function, seizures, tremors
Folic Acid	abnormal cervical cells, anemia, birth defects, heart disease
Inositol	constipation, eczema, elevated cholesterol, gastritis, hypertension
Iron	anemia, brittle nails, hair loss, fatigue, poor immune function, weakness
Potassium	fatigue, irregular heartbeat, irritability, confusion, reduced nerve function, edema
Selenium	cardiovascular disease, depression, fatigue, hair loss, hypothyroidism, lack of libido, memory loss, miscarriage/reproductive disorder, moodiness, poor concentration,

[3] Gilligan MA. Metformin and vitamin B12 deficiency (letter). Arch Intern Med 2002;162:484-5

	poor immune function
Zinc	acne, balding, delayed wound healing, diabetes, irregular menstruation, darkened pigmentation, decreased immunity, frequent infections, loss of taste and smell, painful joints, poor appetite, sexual dysfunction, skin disorders, poor circulation
Magnesium	anorexia, anxiety, asthma, cardiovascular disease, confusion, diabetes, disorientation, fatigue, hyperacidity, hypertension, insomnia, irritability, muscle cramps, nausea, numbness, osteoporosis, painful menstrual cramps, personality changes, rapid heart rate, sensitivity to sound, tingling, vomiting, weakness
CoQ$_{10}$	cardiovascular disease, congestive heart failure, hypertension, muscle weakness
Carnitine	inability to digest fat, muscle weakness, poor athletic performance
vitamin B$_1$ (Thiamine)	anemia, confusion, edema, fatigue, headache, heart failure, impaired sensory perception, irregular heartbeat, loss of appetite, nervousness, sleep disturbance, weakness, weight loss
vitamin B$_2$ (Riboflavin)	burning and itching eyes, depression, dry cracks of the skin and at the corners of the mouth and lips, sensitivity, sore throat, swollen tongue, vision loss, light sensitivity
vitamin B$_3$ (Niacin)	aggression, anorexia, balding, "brain fog," canker sores, cracked and scaly skin, dementia, depression, dermatitis, diarrhea, headaches, indigestion, insomnia, nausea, swelling, vomiting, weakness
vitamin B$_5$ (Pantothenic Acid)	acne, arthritis, constipation, depression, eczema, fatigue, foot pain, gout, graying hair, headache, increased infections, muscle cramps, numbness, "pins & needles" sensation of the skin
vitamin B$_6$ (Pyridoxine)	acne, anemia, blood sugar intolerance, depression, dermatitis, elevated homocysteine (increased risk for cardiovascular disease), fatigue, hyperactivity, hypertension , irritability, nervousness, water retention, weakness
vitamin B$_7$ (Biotin)	anorexia, balding, cradle cap (in newborns), dandruff, decreased appetite, depression, dermatitis, hallucinations, nausea
vitamin B$_9$ (Folate)	anemia, birth defects, cervical abnormalities, depression, diarrhea, drowsiness, elevated homocysteine (increased risk for cardiovascular disease), fatigue, gingivitis, insomnia, irritability, mental illness, slow wound healing, weakness
vitamin B$_{12}$ (Cobalamin)	anemia, confusion, depression, diarrhea, dizziness, drowsiness, easy bruising, elevated homocysteine (increased risk for cardiovascular disease), fatigue, loss of appetite, memory loss, nausea, neurologic changes, peripheral neuropathy (poor nerve function), poor blood clotting, psychosis, sore tongue
vitamin C	bleeding gums, decreased immunity, easy bruising, fatigue, joint

	pain, loose teeth, poor wound healing, scurvy, weight loss
vitamin D	decreased immunity, hearing loss, muscle weakness, osteomalacia (soft bones), osteoporosis (bone loss), rickets (in children)
vitamin E	abnormal heartbeats, anemia, ataxia, male infertility, malnutrition, peripheral neuropathy, poor immune function

Per Natural Medicines Comprehensive Database, 4% of nutrient depletions are rated "major," 44% are rated "moderate," and 36% are rated "insignificant." For the remaining 15%, there is not adequate information to evaluate clinical significance.

If you are currently taking prescription or over-the-counter drugs, especially long term, I strongly encourage you to consult your doctor about possible supplements and nutrition deficiencies. As you can see, drug-induced nutrient deficiency is more common than you might think and what you don't know *can* hurt you. Furthermore, there are numerous cases of prescription-supplement interactions too. In excess amounts, nutrients and vitamins can behave similar to prescription drugs and cause dangerous side effects.

The U.S. recommended daily intake (RDI) is the government's standard of the minimal amount of various nutrients that the body needs to avoid a deficiency state and disease. It is not designed to help people achieve optimal wellness. Since the RDI of nutrients typically applies to a young, healthy individual without chronic medical issues, prescription medications, high stress, or dietary insufficiencies, these recommendations are typically not adequate. For you to maintain an optimal state of health, nutrient supplementation must be designed specifically for you and may require much more than the recommended daily intake. Thus, it is important that you obtain expert advice to help guide you through this new journey. As a foundation, it is essential that you take a multivitamin that is gender and age appropriate, an additional dose of vitamin D_3 of at least 800-1,000 IU, the anti-oxidant Coenzyme Q_{10} (100mg), a balanced and pure essential fatty acid (fish oil or cod liver oil) and a quality probiotic that is high in culture count and that which is tailored to your health conditions. Be mindful of what you eat. Make sure your diet is well balanced, filled with a variety of anti-oxidant rich fruits and vegetables as well as a quality protein source, and supplement this with water and exercise to maintain a healthy weight. A healthy body, mind and spirit all complement one another so you must strive to balance all three. All of these preventative measures will help you to avoid lifestyle related illness so that you can live a longer and healthier life.

Although time and space do not allow me to thoroughly cover all medications and the health issues that are related to nutrient depletion, I have included several references for your use. Unfortunately, very little of this information is taught in traditional medical training and some healthcare providers become very uneasy when their patients ask to discuss supplements. Most office visits are short and many medical professionals find it difficult to include education as part of their practice, especially if their patients are sick. If you find yourself in this situation, do not be discouraged. Try to partner with him/her and request that s/he do additional research or refer you to someone who is more knowledgeable in the area of Integrative Medicine. A provider who has had additional training in this field will combine conventional medical treatments with other therapies that have been proven to be effective and safe. This will result in a whole body approach- not just treating your disease but also treating you, as a whole person.

Ultimately, **your health is your responsibility** and you owe it to yourself to investigate. Armed with this knowledge you can make wise decisions about your well-being. Since life is about choices, make the choice to honor your body, for great care was given to its design.

The bottom line is this...take control of your health - do the research, invest the time and energy to learn more about your body, attend workshops, find competent professionals to work with, and consider discussing your diet with a nutritionist. Most importantly, **take action** and be the unstoppable woman that you are!

Table 2: Prescription and Non-prescription Drugs

DRUGS	U.S. BRAND NAMES	NUTRIENTS DEPLETED	SUPPLEMENTS (ODI***)
Antacids			
Aluminum Hydroxide, Calcium Carbonate, Magnesium Carbonate, Magnesium Trisilicate, Magnesium Oxide and others	Amphogel, Alterngel, Caltrate, Mylanta, Rolaid, Milk of Magnesia and others	Calcium, Folic Acid, Phosphorus	Calcium (800-1,200mg), Phosphorus (800mg), Folic Acid (400 mcg)
Antibiotics			
Cephalosporins, Fluoroquinolones, Isoniazid, Macrolides, Penicillins, Sulfonamides and others	Ancef, Amoxicillin, Ampicillin, Augmentin, Bactrim, Biaxin, Ciprofloxacin, Doxycycline and others	Healthy intestinal bacteria, Biotin, Inositol, vitamin B_1, vitamin B_2, vitamin B_3, vitamin B_6, vitamin B_{12}, vitamin K	Probiotics, Biotin (300-600mcg), Inositol (100mg), B-complex vitamin, vitamin K (30-100mcg)
Anti-thyroid Medications			
Levothyroxine	Levothyroid, Levoxyl, Synthroid and others	Calcium	Calcium (800-1,200mg)
Cardiovascular Medications			
ACE Inhibitors			
Benazepril, Captopril, Enalapril, Fosinopril, Lisinopril and others	Capoten, Monopril, Prinivil, Zestril, Vasotec and others	Zinc	Zinc (25mg-50mg)
Beta Adrenergic Blocking Agents			
Acebutol, Atenolol, Carvedilol, Metoprolol, Propanolol, Sotalol and others	Betapace, Betimol, Bystolic, Coreg, Corgard, Inderal, Lopressor, Levatol, Ocupress, Trandate, Toprol-XL, Tenormin and others	Coenzyme Q_{10}	CoQ_{10} (100-300mg)
HMG-CoA Reductase Inhibitors			
Atorvastatin, Fluvastatin, Lovastatin, Pravastatin,	Crestor, Lescol, Lipitor Mevacor, Pravachol,	Coenzyme Q_{10}	CoQ_{10} (30-360mg)

Rosuvastatin, Simvastatin	Zocor and others		
Diabetes Medications			
Biguanides			
Metformin	Glucophage, Glucovance and others	vitamin B_{12}	vitamin B_{12} (400-2,000mcg)
Sulfonylureas			
Chlorpromamide, Glimepiride, Glipizide, Glyburide and others	Amaryl, DiaBeta, Diabinese, Glucotrol, Glynase, Micronase	CoQ_{10}	CoQ_{10} (30-360 mg)
Corticosteroids			
Betamethasone, Budesonide, Cortisone, Fluticasone, Prednisone and others	Celestone, Cortone Acetate, Decadron, Deltasone, Flovent, Pulmicort and others	Calcium. Folic Acid, Magnesium, Potassium, Selenium, vitamin D, Zinc	Calcium (800-1,200mg), Folic Acid (400 mcg), Magnesium (400-600mg), Potassium 100mg, Selenium (50-200mcg), vitamin D_3 (1,000-2,000IU), Zinc (25-50mg)
Hormone Replacement Therapy & Oral Contraceptives			
Conjugated Estrogen, Esterified Estrogen, Medroxyprogesterone, Ethinyl Estradiol, Norethindrone and others	Alora, Cenestin, Climara, Estinyl, Estrace, Estratab, Femring, Menest, Premarin, Premphase, Prempro, Provera, Camila, Lo-Ovral, Orthonovum, Ortho-cyclen, Necon, Seasonique, Yaz, Yasmin and others	Calcium, Folic Acid, Magnesium, vitamin B_2, vitamin B_6, vitamin B_{12}, vitamin C, vitamin D, Zinc	Calcium (800-1,200mg), Folic Acid (400 mcg), Magnesium (400-600mg), vitamin B_2 (25mg), vitamin B_6 (50mg), vitamin B_{12} (400-2,000mcg), vitamin C (50-1,000mg), vitamin D_3 (1,000-2,000IU)
Thiazide Diuretics			
Hydrochlorothiazide, Methyclothiazide, Indapamide, Metolazone	Enduron, HydroDIURIL, Microzide, Lozol, Zaroxolyn and others	CoQ_{10}, Magnesium, Potassium, Zinc	CoQ_{10} (30-360mg), Magnesium (400-600mg)
Non-Steroidal Anti-inflammatory Medication			
Celecoxib, Diclofenac, Etodolac, Ibuprofen, Naproxen and others	Advil, Aleve, Anaprox,Cambia, Celebrex, Ibuprofen, Lodine, Naprelan, Naprosyn, Motrin	Folic Acid, Iron, vitamin C	Folic Acid (400mcg), Iron (15-30mg), vitamin C (1,000-5,000mg)
Proton Pump Inhibitors			
Esomeprazole, Lansoprazole, Omeprazole, Pantoprazole	Aciphex, Losec, Nexium, Prevacid, Pantoloc, Prilosec,	Calcium, vitamin B_{12}	Calcium (800-1200mg), vitamin B_{12} (400-

278

	Protonix and others		2,000mcg)
Tricyclic Antidepressants			
Amitriptyline, Amoxapine,Clomipramine, Desipramine, Doxepin, Imipramine, Nortriptyline and others	Anafranil, Asendin, Aventyl, Elavil, Endep, Norpramin, Pamelor, Sinequan and others	CoQ$_{10}$, vitamin B$_2$	CoQ$_{10}$ (30-360mg), vitamin B$_2$ (25mg)
Miscellaneous			
Acetaminophen	Tylenol, Paracetamol	Coenzyme Q$_{10}$, Glutathione,	CoQ$_{10}$ (30-360mg), N-acetylcysteine (500-3,000mg)
Aspirin	Ecotrin, Bufferin, and others	Folic Acid, Iron, vitamin C, Potassium, Zinc	Folic Acid (400mcg), Iron (15-30mg), vitamin C (1,000-5,000mg), Potassium 100mg, Zinc (25-50 mg)

***(ODI) Optimal Daily Intake- a safe dose range for general optimal health-may vary according to a person's age, sex, race and health status. Increased levels may be required to correct deficiency.

Consult your healthcare provider before initiating supplements. Some supplements may require divided doses.

Who is at Higher Risk for Drug-Nutrient Depletion?

- Young children
- The elderly
- Pregnant Women
- People with multiple health problems
- Lower income populations
- Isolation
- People who have a poor diet
- People taking more than one medication at the same time
- People who drink alcohol excessively
- People who smoke excessively
- People who are not taking medication as prescribed
- People taking over-the-counter medications with prescription medications

How to Lower the Risk of Drug-Nutrient Interactions

- Eat a well-balanced diet and avoid missing meals.
- Take prescription medications as directed.
- Read warning labels on both prescription and over-the-counter medications.
- Do not take medications that were not prescribed for you.
- Do not take over-the-counter medications on a chronic basis.
- Tell your physician about everything you are taking, including over-the-counter medications, supplements and herbal products.
- Inform your provider about any new symptoms that you are experiencing while taking medications.
- Supplement your prescriptions.
- Find a provider who understands nutrition and drug-nutrient interactions.

Resources:

- A-Z Guide to Drug-Herb-Vitamin Interactions: Improve Your Health and Avoid Side Effects When Using Common Medications and Natural Supplements Together, Alan R Gaby, M.D. (Editor), Forrest Batz, Pharm.D. (Editor), Rick Chester, R.PH., N.D. (Editor)
- Before You Take That Pill: Why the Drug Industry May be Bad for Your Health: Risks and Side Effects You Won't Find on the Label of Commonly Prescribed Drugs, Vitamins and Supplements, J. Douglas Bremner, MD
- Drug-Induced Nutrient Depletion Handbook. Lexi-Comp; 2nd Edition., 2001 Pelton, Lavalle, Hawkins, Krinsky.
- Drugs That Deplete - Nutrients That Heal: A Review of Drug-Induced Nutrient Depletion Handbook, 1999-2000. Life Extension Magazine, July 2000.
- Natural Medicines Comprehension Database www.naturaldatabase.com
- The New Nutrition: Medicine for the Millennium, Michael Colgan
- The Real Vitamin and Mineral Book, 4th edition: The Definitive Guide to Designing Your Personal Supplement Program, Nancy Pauling Bruning, Shari Lieberman
- What You Must Know About Vitamins, Minerals, Herbs & More Choosing the Nutrients That Are Right For You, Pamela Wartian Smith, M.D., MPH

References:

1. Alpers DH, Clause RE, Stenson WF. *Manual of Nutritional Therapeutics, 2nd ed.* Little, Brown and Company, 1988.

2. Bliznakov EG, Wilkins DJ. Biochemical and clinical consequences of inhibiting coenzyme Q10 biosynthesis by lipid-lowering HMG-CoA reductase inhibitors (Statins): a critical overview. *Adv Ther.* Jul/Aug 1998;15(4):218-228.

3. Elin RJ. Magnesium: the fifth but forgotten electrolyte. Am J Clin Pathol. 1994;102(5):616–622.

4. Ghirlanda G, Oradei A, Manto A, Lippa S, Uccioli L, Caputo S, Greco AV, Littarru GP. Evidence of plasma CoQ10-lowering effect by HMG-CoA reductase inhibitors: a double-blind, placebo-controlled study. *J Clin Pharmacol.* 1993.Mar;33(3):226-229.

5. Langsjoen PH, Langsjoen AM. The clinical use of HMG CoA-reductase inhibitors and the associated depletion of coenzyme Q10: a review of animal and human publications. *Biofactors*, 2003;18(1-4):101-11.

6. Long PJ, Shannon B. *Focus on Nutrition* Englewood Cliffs, NJ: Prentice-Hall, Inc., 1983.

7. Pelton, La Valle, et al. Drug-Induced Nutrient Depletion Handbook. *Lexi-Comp Clinical Reference Library*. 1999-2000.

8. Pressman AH. *Clinical Assessment of Nutritional Status: A Working Manual*. Management Enterprises, 1982.

9. Reavley N. *New Encyclopedia of Vitamins, Minerals, Supplements and Herbs*. New York: M. Evans & Co. Inc., 1998.

10. Rybacki JJ, Long JW. *The Essential Guide to Prescription Drugs*. Harper Resource, 2001.

11. Shils ME, Olson JA. Modern Nutrition in Health and Disease. 8th ed.Philadelphia, Pa.: Lea & Febiger; 1994.

12. Smith, Pamela Wartian, M.D., MPH   What You Must Know About Vitamins, Minerals, Herbs & More Choosing the Nutrients That Are Right For You

13. Watts GF, Castelluccio C, Rice-Evans C, Taub NA, Baum H, Quinn PJ. Plasma coenzyme Q (ubiquinone) concentrations in patients treated with simvastatin. *J Clin Pathol.* Nov 1993;46(11):1055-1057.

 Peggy Smith was born on February 26, 1924 from Bristol, England. She came from a very poor family living with her mother, brother, and sister. Peggy never knew her father. Yet somehow, her mother, with the aid of the family's social worker, managed to get enough money together to purchase a second-hand piano.

Growing up, this little girl recalls the whistling sound of bombs being dropped from enemy airplanes, and the horrifying sound as they would hit the ground and explode, leaving massive death and destruction behind. After each bombing raid ended, they would then exit the bomb shelters and try to resume a "normal" life.

Peggy received an honors certificate from the London College of Music, the largest specialist music and performing arts institution in the U.K., at the tender age of 12! Today, Peggy is busier than ever. She performs at Edward Hospital in Naperville, Delnor Hospital in Geneva, Friendship Village Retirement Center, all in the state of Illinois. In a single year, she totaled more than 100 performances, all at no charge. In facilities where residents are confined, Peggy provides a complimentary CD of her music. Her first CD was recorded April 8th, 2011 and every one of the 17 tracks were 1st takes, with no edits or redo's.

This humble, kind, and loving woman is cherished, and is an inspiration to all who meet her. But her biggest fans are her four sons: Brian, John, Budd, and Bob!

Contact information:

Budd Smith: 630-393-1545
budnkak@aol.com

Chapter 23

Learning What Really Matters
Story of: Peggy Smith
As told to: John Burek, J.D.

Spring does not mean the end of all bad weather, nor does peace mean the end of all things harsh and bad. So it was in England after World War I, the Great War, the "War to end all Wars". Wales may be picturesque for visitors, but the economic realities were nowhere near as nice. Peggy left Wales with her mother Mary, her brother Leonard, and sister Iris, known to friends and family as Babe, when she was ten years of age. Economic realities weren't rosy in England, but the chance at a better life overcame any hesitation that they felt.

The family left without Dad, who had gone missing some years before. While single parent families are common today, a family headed by a young woman was not the norm in those days. The weight of those times left Peggy feeling sorry for her mother, and she tried to help make-up for those hardships by taking on a role usually filled by someone older. She became a helper, more than a child. But events were taking place in lands far away which would shape her life in a profound way.

Peggy always had the knack of making friends. Her easy smile and frequent laugh made her popular in the neighborhood. One of those friends, Lisa, had a brother, and he had a piano. He offered to teach her, and she gladly accepted. She soon had developed the beginnings of her unique play by ear style. Her mother, Mary Ann Webb, had always wanted to learn piano, but Mary Ann's father told her she must play violin, instead. That desire didn't go away, but lay dormant until her mother finally got a piano in Bristol.

Peggy showed her some of what she could do, and soon Peggy studied music at the London College of Music. While that helped her learn technique, the music was all classical, and Peggy had already encountered, and fell in love with Big Band music. Those bands from across the sea, Glen Miller, Artie Shaw, and Benny Goodman, among others, lit a fire in Peggy that burns bright until this day.

That music helped in other ways. While working in a bag factory helped the war effort in the early days of World War II, and also provided a steady paycheck, it wasn't always challenging for Peggy. It did provide a paycheck that helped her raise her son Brian, while her husband Arthur was away in the war. She looked forward to his regular letters, until they abruptly stopped. It took three weeks for her to hear that lonely knock on the door, with expressions about sorrow for her loss. So when she heard about an opening at Bristol Airplane Company (the fore-runner of British Airways), she took the chance and applied.

How much her musical talent helped her get that job is unclear, but while she worked there, she played during her lunch break. Her playing so moved people, that soon Peggy became featured at Frenchay Hospital, playing for the soldiers. That certainly caught the attention of Dorothea Lane, field director of the American Red Cross. Peggy soon was playing for the "walking wounded", those people whose wounds lasted far beyond the war. It was at Frenchay Hospital that Peggy met her second husband, Jordet (Smitty). The Americans needed a hospital for their rapidly increasing casualties, and in co-operation with the English government, Frenchay became the hospital/home away from home for the Americans. Peggy soon discovered that the music wasn't simply the escape that she enjoyed, it often meant far more to the men. For them, it was an escape from pain, and disability. For some, it re-called a simple, better time; a time without the scars of war. Eyes mist over, and legs that may not otherwise work as they once had, move in time with the music. The power of music had never been more pronounced, and it formed a pattern of Peggy using music to give back to the world that she still enjoys today. While the wounds today are often from fighting a losing battle against the ravages of time, the effect is no less profound. Little has changed in people's reaction to her music over the last fifty years. Requests still flow from the crowds, seeking to remember happier times. Seldom is there a dry eye in the house. Never are people not moved.

A new country meant new challenges. Things were more spread out in Tulsa OK. than back home, and it so became apparent that relying on one driver wasn't possible. So at age forty, Peggy needed to learn to drive. Driving can seem unnatural under the best of conditions, but with small children and a house to run, Peggy's concentration was tested to the limits. But persistence and determination won out, and she got her coveted license. But the thrill of getting that new bit of freedom was short-lived. Only months after getting her license, Peggy heard one of the most dreaded five letter words that then existed; polio.

Smitty got the diagnosis just months before the new miracle drug developed by Dr. Jonas Saulk was released. Some today don't remember how devastating such a diagnosis was; it could be a death sentence, or spending a life in an iron lung, unable to breathe on your own, ever again. Smitty was told that his paralysis was permanent, and that he would never walk again. He told the doctors that they were dead wrong, and he began the long, arduous process of re-learning how to make his limbs work. Not much was known about polio then, and he had to remain in the hospital. Peggy brought the kids to see him every week. But seeing him was all they were able to do. The hospital refused to allow them to be in the hospital with their Dad, so they stayed outside, and taking turns, were placed on Peggy's shoulders, so they could waive to their Dad.

Whatever tears Peggy shed would never be known; they were a private matter. It was hard enough on the kids to have Dad out of the house; there was no reason for them to see their Mother's grief, too. So, with her newly minted license, Peggy ran the house, and took care of the kids by herself. Her source of comfort in those times, as it had been through-out her life, was the piano. She played for the kids, and for herself. Music filled the house, and brought a warmth that was sorely needed. Smitty was up and on crutches within a year, and he soon threw them away. But it took ten hard years of work before he could throw out the brace he had to wear, fulfilling his vow to the doctors.

Those years also saw a change in the financial fortunes for the Smith family. After years of running a very successful car wash, Smitty came home one day, and announced he had purchased a restaurant. Not an on-going operation; that would have been too easy. This one, The Lighthouse, and been vacant for years, and it took the whole family many months of work to get it back in shape. Although the restaurant was Smitty's vision, much of the work fell on Peggy. She cooked breakfast and lunch, then went home to take care of the family, before returning to cook dinner, bar tend, before playing piano or organ until closing. Sometimes a drummer from England would sit it, and sometimes a bass player. The place soon became as well known for its music, as Peggy's famous (and authentic) fish and chips.

Smitty passed in 1996, and Peggy could have spent her time quietly, being a doting mother and grandmother. But when her son Budd was named district manager, and was transferred to Milwaukee, Peggy agreed to purchase his business. Starting over at age sixty-two didn't faze Peggy at all. Never one to be a passive manager, Peggy set out to learn everything she could about the business, taking and passing all of the grueling insurance exams she needed to get the licenses she would need. She ran that business so successfully that she was named the Distinguished Business Person of the Year from her adopted home town in 2004 at age **eighty**. She continues to get inquiries from her former clients to this day, though she finally did turn the running of the business back to Budd in 2009.

That didn't mean that she was retired, however, it just meant there was more time for music. With Budd making the arrangements, Peggy played at over one hundred engagements in 2011, and recorded her first CD. She plans to double that in 2012. She still plays by ear, and has thousands of songs in her memory bank. Requests seldom find her unprepared. The favorites still seem to be the classics she learned from the radio many years ago; she adds newer songs to challenge herself, and to keep current.

After spending time interviewing Ms. Smith for this book, I had a chance to talk to her about how she managed to persevere through such extraordinary hardships. I asked her what advice she would give to a woman of twenty, starting out today. This is how the conversation went:

She said, "Never give up."

"It can't be as simple as that," I replied.

"No, of course not" she smiled, "but if you forget to follow that, all of the other rules won't mean anything."

"What other rules?"

"Well, maybe "rules" isn't the right word. Maybe "practices" would be better. They are guides for your journey. There are four I found helped me the most."

She then told me what they were, and asked me to share them with you. I have taken the liberty of paraphrasing our discussion, for purposes of time.

1. BE TRUE TO YOUR PASSION

Everyone has a passion. Some have more than one, but that passion is there. Too many people, however, are convinced to push them aside, often under the pre-text of having to "grow up", or move on in the real world. Peggy found her passion early in life, her love of music, and expressing that by playing the piano. That passion was a great source of comfort for her and her family, and certainly helped her through the more difficult times. Having a piano was a prerequisite for her later life, especially in her second marriage. Playing the piano allowed her to give not only to her family, but the customers in the restaurant, and later patients in the nursing homes or retirement centers.

Not everyone has a musical calling. So what! Whatever activity brings you pleasure, it allows you to connect to your inner self and it has value. It doesn't matter if you bake, or read, or write, or garden, or run or just like to spend time with your girl friends, all are equally valid. Today, even more than the past, it is easy to get over-whelmed by events. Privacy is largely a thing of the past.

Everyone is now accessible seven days a week. Whether you tweet or text, IM or Facebook, the times when you have several hours of consecutive, uninterrupted time are few and far between. Having that activity that allows you to escape the madding crowd, re-connect with yourself, and re-charge those internal batteries is critical. The world won't stop and create time for you, so if you don't do it for yourself, it will never happen, and a unique part of yourself will slowly suffocate and be lost. Events can always expand to fill available time; put time aside for yourself first, and you won't be disappointed.

2.   OWN YOUR LIFE

Peggy's mother had an extraordinarily difficult life. Raising young children as a single parent in an era that didn't look upon that as an acceptable alternative life style, made a dramatic impact on her. She sought approval in many ways, likely not even knowing that that was the deeper meaning of the act or gesture. This in turn, led Peggy to try and assume a larger role in protecting and nurturing her mother. Peggy felt like she was older than her years, and she probably was, but that isn't conducive for anyone's well-being. Married at eighteen, widowed by twenty, with a young child, it would have been easy to throw up her hands, and complain about the bad hand that had been dealt her. "There are things in life you just can't change, so you **must** accept them," she has said. She lived those words, and that made all of the difference. She didn't have an advanced degree, but she didn't care. She did the best with what she had, with not a minute of time wasted on regret. Because she never wasted any time on complaining, she had more time to do what was needed.

Everyone has something that could have been better. "If I was taller, smarter, better-looking, thinner, richer, then I would be happier." All of these wishes/complaints serve only one end; they give an excuse for you to not do more, accomplish more, be more. And none of them matter in the end. Make a list of all of the things that make up "you." Be honest, and be complete. Then think about each and every point, and learn to accept all of them. It doesn't mean you can't work to make some areas better, but it does mean you can't let any of them stop you from going out and doing what needs to be done. Time wasted on those parts of you which could have been better, is time you will never get back. So grieve if you must, cry if you want, scream if that works for you, then take that sheet of paper, and burn it. Never let anything on that list ever bother you again. They are now in the past. The future belongs to you if you want it.

3. YOU ARE NEVER TOO OLD TO START

Peggy got started in insurance when she was in her sixties. People probably told her that she was too old, and that insurance takes years to develop. She didn't listen, and ran a successful agency for many years. She received the Distinguished Business Person from her town at eighty! If she had just listened to conventional wisdom, none of that would have happened. Who cares how many years you have left, if they are good years! Whether you have one year or thirty, make each one the best you can. The simple act of **doing** will makes things better. The feeling of accomplishing something never gets dimmer with age, in some cases it gets accelerated. If you are the oldest "new" agent, so what? You just broke ground for someone else. In these increasingly fractious times, people will likely have more than one or two careers. Starting later to achieve that goal means nothing. In fact, that extra experience may give you a leg up on some of the kids. Peggy recorded her first CD at eighty-seven, and will be going back into the studio later this year to record her second CD. Tell her she's too old, and she'll smile at you, just before she smacks you on the back of the head.

4. SILENCE CAN BE A DREAM KILLER

Be accountable to others. Peggy told her son Budd about her dreams to play for others less kindly dealt with by the world; he took her up on her challenge and began to schedule dates for her to perform, letting her share her gift with the world. She did have one stipulation; every performance had to be free. In 2011, Peggy played in over one hundred engagements, and recorded her first CD. In the coming year, it looks like that may double. If she had never talked to others about her dreams, they would have remained dreams only. Find five people you trust, and talk to them about what you want to accomplish, and how and when you want to get there. Ideas can be inter-active. Your team may have options for you that you never knew of. They may be able to put you in touch with others that can help. They may have other ideas. At the very least, you are forced to clarify your thoughts so you can express your goals to others. Then, follow-up at least monthly. Even if all you have to share that month is what you consider failures, the mere fact that it is shared with others will not only reduce its power to slow you down, but you will have created an instant support team to get you back on track. Never feel that you have to do this alone, you don't. The more you involve others, the better chance you have for success.

All of these guidelines can and will work, but only if you remember the most important three words; NEVER GIVE UP. Once you truly internalize those words, and make them a core part of you, you will be on the path for success. The four rules Peggy gives above will make that path a little straighter, a little smoother. You are still responsible for doing the work, but you don't have to do it alone. And that's how being unstoppable is truly defined!